In-between Cultures

On the Migratory Artistic Identity of Sidi Larbi Cherkaoui and Akram Khan

Guy Cools

Antennae
Valiz, Amsterdam

In-between Dance Cultures
On the Migratory Artistic Identity of
Sidi Larbi Cherkaoui and Akram Khan

Guy Cools

Contents

Introduction

> In order not to diminish the thought of the present, one shouldn't take the words that come out of it as an absolute truth, as dogmas one has to follow. The ink can never replace the truth of the lived instant, of its context, but it might simulate or even better stimulate it.[1]

I remember from my own formative years as a young theatre and dance critic at the Flemish newspaper *De Morgen* (1986–1990) that I was advised by some of my older colleagues (for example the theatre critic Wim Van Gansbeke) that art criticism is first and foremost a literary genre and that it should try to absorb and translate some of the formal qualities of the works of art it discusses.

This book is the result of being, for more than fifteen years, a privileged witness to two artists who have, individually and through their exchanges, defined the first decade of twenty-first century contemporary dance history: Belgian-Moroccan choreographer Sidi Larbi Cherkaoui and British-Bengali choreographer Akram Khan.[2] Their public careers as contemporary choreographers began at roughly the same time, around the shift into the second millennium. Larbi created his first group piece, *Rien de Rien*, in 2000. Akram, who was already an acclaimed performer of Indian Kathak dance, created his first group piece, *Rush*, in the same year. I was present at the first steps that these two artists took in their choreographic careers, and at the moment when these careers converged.

Works of art should speak for themselves, regardless of the autobiography or 'identity' of the artist. But when, as in the case of Sidi Larbi Cherkaoui and Akram Khan, artists develop their identity as a major theme, it becomes relevant again as a possible entry into the work.[3]

I owe it to my subjects to take up the challenge that I was given as a young critic and to practice the same polyphonic eclecticism that marks the work of Sidi Larbi Cherkaoui, or to allow myself to be confused in-between different voices, a creative principle applied by Akram Khan. This book mixes at least three distinctive voices: a personal, autobiographical one; an academic one that synthesizes the existing critical discourse; and an artistic one having accompanied them as a dance dramaturge enabling me to offer privileged insight into the creative process of two of the twenty-first century's most remarkable choreographers. While one voice becomes dominant in each of the following chapters, the other two always resonate in the background, since these voices are impossible to separate completely. Moreover, they are in dialogue with others throughout this book, primarily of course those of Larbi and Akram.

In the first chapter I talk about some of my own experience as a 'migrating body.' It is a story that is formative for my own identity and has brought me to this point: writing this book in Berlin while living in Vienna and working as a 'dance nomad' in a multitude of countries. I am only able to live this life thanks to a huge support system of family, friends, and colleagues. I want to acknowledge all the artists—choreographers, dancers, and artistic collaborators—who have contributed to the creations discussed in this book, in particular Sidi Larbi Cherkaoui and Akram Khan, the two protagonists who are also both generous artists and good friends of mine. They wouldn't have arrived where they are in their career without being in continuous artistic exchange with other artists (exchanges which, in fact, they often initiate themselves) and without the generous support of a number of people accompanying their careers. I would like to mention a few of these people who have supported them, as I also value and cherish their friendship and support: Herwig Onghena and Lieven Thyrion of Les Ballets C de la B in Ghent, Farooq Chaudhry of the Akram Khan Company in London, Emma Gladstone who used to work at Sadler's Wells London, and An-Marie Lambrechts of Toneelhuis in Antwerp.

The second chapter focuses on how critical theory has addressed the notion of identity, and on how both Sidi Larbi Cherkaoui and Akram Khan have consciously embedded their own artistic output into this discourse. I was able to deepen my understanding of and insight into this subject during my residency as a fellow at the International Research Center 'Interweaving Performance Cultures' at Freie Universität in Berlin. The staff at the centre and all the other fellows have provided a stimulating intellectual environment, allowing me to finish this book. I am particularly grateful to Dr. Christel Weiler and Holger Hartung for their hospitality, support, and guidance. I am equally grateful to Dr. Pascal Gielen, my colleague at the research institute Arts in Society at the Fontys School of Fine and Performing Arts for supporting the publication of this book, and to Astrid Vorstermans and Pia Pol of the publishing house Valiz in Amsterdam for generously seeing it through to its realization.

The third chapter discusses individual creations in which the topic of an identity in-between cultures has been a major source and theme for Sidi Larbi Cherkaoui and Akram Khan separately, but also collaboratively as in their work *zero degrees* (2005). I try to give insight into their creative processes from the witness position of the dramaturge. I complement this subjective perspective with fragments of performance and reception analysis. I am grateful to Lisa Marie Bowler, who has been my language editor for these past years, and to Karthika Nair, who, as a fellow writer and collaborator of both Larbi and Akram, has been one of my first critical readers, together with Holger Hartung and Lin Snelling.

In the concluding chapter, I allow my own voice to become more dominant again in order to reassert my belief in dialogue as the essence of dramaturgical practice and the only way to engage with the world and the Other, accepting that our mutual understanding will always be only partial. It is in the in-between of listening and articulating that there is a potential for the creation of a much needed new social imagery. Watching and listening to 'migrating bodies' like those of Sidi Larbi Cherkaoui and Akram Khan can guide us in this dialogical practice. To paraphrase author Gary Zukav, they are 'dancing Wu Li masters,' reenergizing not only their art form but also the larger social environment of which they are part. I only found the energy and stamina to finish this book because of the relentless support of my wife Stephanie Cumming, who also gave me the necessary space to embark on this journey.

Both writing and reading are not necessarily linear processes. Written texts only create the illusion of linearity. I have tried to conceive each section of this book in such a way that it might also be read and appreciated independently. I would like to invite my readers to create their own journey, following their own interests. Safe travels.

Guy Cools
Vienna and Berlin, 2015

Notes

1   Cherkaoui 2006b, p. 1. Wherever the
    sources are Dutch, French, or German,
    the quotes are my own translations.
2   In the whole book, I will allow myself to alter-
    nate freely between their full names and
    the more familiar Larbi and Akram.
3   We might expect, and this is already to
    some extent visible, that as their career
    moves forward they will refer less to their
    identity as their main source of inspiration.

Aren't We All Migrating Bodies?

To be embodied is to participate in a migration from one body form to another. Each of us is a nomad, a wave that has duration for a time and then takes on a new somatic shape. This perpetual transformation is the subject of all myth.[1]

Moving Forward and Backward[2]

In our deepest natures, we are frontier-crossing beings. We know this by the stories we tell ourselves; for we are story-telling animals, too.[3]

'Moving' may be one of the most important characteristics of our human condition. From birth to death, we constantly and uninterruptedly move. Even in moments of rest and sleep, our bodies and minds continue to function, to make unconscious journeys into the past and its memories or the future and its desires. A lot of those movements are conditioned, genetically inherited from our parents and ancestors, going as far back as the animal state; determined by our gender, which is not a fixed physical entity but a fluid, dynamic force field of complementary or conflicting energies; and activated and actualized by the place and time we are born and grow up in—its climate, its food, its language, its educational system, its social, economic, political, and cultural context. 'The body doesn't lie' is the recurrent motto in *Blood Memory* (1991), Martha Graham's autobiography, in which she expresses the ancient idea that the body is the memory bank of everything we have lived, felt, thought.

Our movements determine the limits of our existence, but they also create opportunities. In our journey through life, we all arrive at a crossroads or at frontiers that offer us the option to change directions, leaping forward or stepping backward. There are no wrong choices, but every choice has its own consequences. We can learn from both a leap forward or retreat backward. As to the latter, I agree with Hans Magnus Enzensberger that retreat is a more heroic act than conquest.[4] But we do need freedom of choice.

'Freedom of movements across frontiers' is the main theme of Salman Rushdie's lecture and later essay 'Step Across This Line.' In it he discusses a whole series of journeys, both individual and collective, ancient and contemporary, real or imagined, in which freedom of movement, also 'to step across the line,' is essential: 'The crossing of borders, of language, geography and culture; the examination of the permeable frontier between the universe of things and deeds and the universe of the imagination; the lowering of the intolerable frontiers created by the world's many different kinds of Thought Policemen.'[5] I would like to add one of my own accounts to his collection of stories, 'the tracks we leave behind.'

From 1990 until 2002, I commute on a daily basis by train from Antwerp, the city I am born and live in (in my ancestor's house), to Ghent, where I am responsible for the contemporary dance program at Arts Centre Vooruit.[6] Antwerp and Ghent are two major Flemish cities, only sixty kilometres apart, but separated by our major river, the Scheldt. For twelve years the river is the main border I cross, every day, forward and backward, moving while sitting on a train.[7]

Living in a globalized world where the tensions between the global and the local seem to increase every day, the dilemmas and crises related to the formation of my own identity seemed only minimally conditioned by my GPS, my global position—that is, being Western European and having to find a personal answer to both the threat of an economic, political, and finally also cultural Americanization and the historical guilt and debt to the rest of the postcolonial world.

The so often mediatized and politically abused question of my Belgian/Flemish identity—living on the historical and geographical border between Roman and Germanic cultures and languages, a border between forest and plains—never feels problematic. On the contrary, having worked in the arts for most of my professional life, I have come to understand and appreciate this mixed identity as the basis for our rich and creative cultural and artistic landscape. When I am once mockingly questioned by the Greek minister of culture about the nature of Belgian cultural tradition and identity, I immediately retort that it simply has to be the playful and visionary hyper-real hybrid of 'sur-realism' from Pieter Breughel via James Ensor and René Magritte to Marcel Broodthaers and Panamarenko.

As for the religious border to the north, which already in the sixteenth century made the Netherlands independent and Protestant and kept us Flemings Catholic and dominated by other cultures and languages (with French being the major one) well into the twentieth century—I always feel this put us in the enviable position of the second child, the 'underdog.' The 'slowness' of our cultural maturity and independence allows us to learn from the mistakes of our 'role model,' the Dutch 'polder model,' imitating only its obvious qualities but rejecting its excesses, such as for instance its politically correct rigidity and over-organization.

No, in my personal journey, the smallest geographical opposition—between two Flemish cities, separated by a river—has the greatest impact. 'To be from over the water' remains a blasphemous expression labelling you a stranger, an outsider and intruder, not belonging and never being fully accepted by the locals. My first great love, who has been my partner for almost fifteen years, comes 'from over the water,' and so do I, from my in-laws' point of view. And although this is not the only reason why we eventually separate, it does put a lot of unnecessary, external pressure on our relationship from day one.

My own, daily commute 'forward,' which draws an individual meridian from Antwerp to Ghent, coincides with a larger, historical and collective meridian which summarizes part of the history and culture of the 'Low Countries.' As a result of changes in the natural environment or political and religious events, the centre of the economic and cultural life in the Middle Ages first moves east and then 'goes' north. Bruges is the first economic and cultural centre. Its medieval character as the 'Venice of the North' remains intact, as visited by writer Marguerite Yourcenar's Zeno. But when the river connecting the city to the sea dries up, the economic centre moves east, first to Ghent and later to Antwerp, 'ending' in Amsterdam after the religious wars at the end of the sixteenth century, and thus making the seventeenth century the Dutch 'Golden Age,' partially financed by colonial exploitation. In painting, a similar journey in time would take us from the Flemish Primitives with Van Eyck's *Adoration of the Mystic Lamb* (1430-1432), kept in the Cathedral of Ghent, via Rubens's *Crucifixion* (1618-1620) in Antwerp to Rembrandt's *The Night Watch* (1642) in Amsterdam.

Even today the 'medieval' competition between cities remains an important factor of political, economic, and cultural life—not only in Flanders, but also in Germany, Italy, or Spain, to name but a few countries. If in fact there is any ground for collective stereotypes, it lies neither in Belgian, nor Flemish nature, but in the shared values and characteristics of the *burghers* of a city.

Ghent's inhabitants are nicknamed *stroppendragers* [noose wearers], in memory of their resistance to the centralized power of Charles I. Today's artistic community still has the reputation of being anarchic, while in Antwerp, their peers—living up to their nickname *sinjoren* [*des seigneurs*, lords]—tend to be more full of themselves, more serious, not to say megalomaniac.

My personal, daily journey forward in life coincides with a historical journey backward. Both in my native city and the city to whose cultural life I contribute, I am an outsider, a stranger. 'Not belonging to any place, any time, any love. A lost origin, the impossibility to take root, a rummaging memory, the present in abeyance. The space of the foreigner is a moving train, a plane in flight, the very transition that precludes stopping.'[8] In *Strangers to Ourselves* (1991), Julia Kristeva uses the history of Western civilization to describe the position of the outsider: its strengths, how essential it is to have an overview, always from a distance, how this lonely freedom gives outsiders the opportunity to move, to make a new synthesis, but also how it renders them weak, dependent, in a new master and slave dialectic, on the hospitality of the landlord; unable to speak one's mother tongue and never being entirely fluent in the new language, 'silence becomes their element, between two languages.'

Both Rushdie and Kristeva consider the problematic challenges offered by this in-between state to also be creative opportunities,[9] most noticeable in the aspect of language. 'Anyone who has crossed a language frontier will readily understand that such a journey involves a form of shape-shifting or self-translation. The change of language changes us. All languages permit slightly varying forms of thought, imagination, and play.'[10] Whereas in my Antwerp dialect they say 'it is great,' in Ghent they will say 'it is wise'—both used in the sense of 'how fantastic.'

Belonging to a very small language community where local dialects are still very much alive and quite different from village to village, where everybody learns more than one foreign language from an early age, I do believe that the key to bridging the local and the global lies in 'translation' as described for instance by George Steiner in *After Babel* (1975). It would follow that the basic opposition in Rushdie's *The Satanic Verses* (1988) is neither between religions, nor cultures, but between 'two fundamentally different types of Self': wishing 'to remain an untranslated man' versus 'a willing re-invention.'[11]

'Exile always involves a shattering of the former body.'[12] What is true for language is also true for the body. Having had the privilege of working with some of the greatest choreographers and dancers of our time, I have come to understand and appreciate dance as a privileged art form, in which we can 'move forward and backward' without the functional border-crossing impediments to which we were conditioned, to learn about the disharmonies of our body, the 'strangers in ourselves.'

Inspired by my yoga practice among other things, I eventually stop my twelve-year commute from one city to another to retreat even further, to make time for more private introspection, and to take the time and space to travel into my own body, to understand and bridge some of its ancient 'gaps.' My yoga practice makes me aware of how my identity is shaped somatically by the energetic polarities of my body, and how I can be transformed by physically exploring and understanding them. In the second chapter I will discuss some of the main critical theories of the notion of cultural identity. Most of these theories, however, remain language-based. Dance can offer an alternative or complementary view, one that also includes somatic knowledge.[13]

Becoming a Migrating Body

> The migrant's sense of being rootless of living between worlds, between a lost past and a non-integrated present, is perhaps the most fitting metaphor of this (post)modern condition.[14]

I write the above in early 2003 in preparation for a large event I curate in Montreal, Canada. *Vooruit Danse en Avant* is my final project for Arts Centre Vooruit. It introduces for the first time a number of European choreographers to Montreal, including Sidi Larbi Cherkaoui with *Foi* (2003) and Akram Khan with a program of his early solo works. In between their performances Larbi and Akram also find some time to go into the studio to start researching and sharing material for what is to become *zero degrees* (2005). As part of the event, I also co-curate an international, UNESCO-supported symposium with Andrée Martin, *Territoires en Mouvance*. It is the first time I reflect and write on the issue of how an individual artistic identity dialogues with the identity of a certain place or territory.

I decide to retreat from my work and the responsibilities attached to it—a retreat that is mainly inspired and induced by the needs of my body to heal from older traumas. But this retreat also creates the necessary space to reinvent myself as a dance curator to become a dance dramaturge, becoming more closely involved with the creative processes of some of the artists I admire. And it also liberates me to actually move and immigrate to Canada. During the months I spend in Montreal preparing the event, I deepen my relationship with its dance community, and also fall in love again and decide to apply for the status of 'permanent resident,' establishing myself in Montreal from August 2004 onward.

I am migrating under the best possible circumstances: from Western Europe to North America before the global crisis of 2008, to a city where I have a huge network of both personal and professional contacts, with the prospect of a new job and a new partner. Still the whole process is psychologically very difficult. In the nine months that pass between the decision and the actual 'moving,' I have to completely uproot myself, say farewell to family, friends, and colleagues, get rid of most of my personal belongings (of which my library carefully collected over a lifetime is the hardest to part with) and go through the demanding administrative Canadian immigration process, which includes health checks for potential lung diseases and AIDS—even for some of my family members who aren't going to accompany me. The culmination point of this process happens when, having finally arrived in Montreal, I have to hand in my Belgian identity card. In exchange, the Canadian status of 'permanent resident' allows me to be tolerated as a privileged outsider with certain benefits (such as a work permit and social security) and obligations (such as paying taxes), but no citizenship.

Eventually the new job and the new relationship don't turn out to be long-lasting, so that while living in Canada from 2004 till 2010 I regularly return to Europe to work as a freelance dance dramaturge. In 2005 I accompany Sidi Larbi Cherkaoui and Akram Khan's creation of *zero degrees* and in the following years I work with each of them on at least three other productions: *Myth* (2007), *Apocrifu* (2007), and *Origine* (2008) with Sidi Larbi Cherkaoui and *Sacred Monsters* (2006), *bahok* (2008), and *in-i* (2008) with Akram Khan. I am enjoying the privileged life of the Western international dance nomad living and working on at least two continents. But as Kristeva states in *Strangers to Ourselves,* once you have gone through the experience of uprooting your-self, you will never fully settle again. I also experience that even in Canada a first generation immigrant will never have full access to the same social and economic opportunities that are available to Canadian citizens.

In *The Foreigner* (2011), Richard Sennett locates the birth of modern forms of nationalism in the revolutions of 1848. He writes that 'nationality becomes an anthropological phenom-enon' in which a collective identity is defined by shared everyday rituals and customs, 'by the manners and mores of a "volk": the food people eat, how they move when they dance, the dialects they speak, the precise forms of their prayers.'[15] They are enactments of a particular territory, so that 'territory becomes synonymous with identity.'

As a result, the displacement of the foreigner, whether immigrant, exile or expatriate, obliges him or her to engage in a dialogue between aspects of his own identity (such as class, race, or gender) and this 'anthropological identity' of a nation. The nation, for a person who has become a foreigner, poses two dangers: 'the danger of forgetting through assimilation or the danger of remem-bering and getting stuck in nostalgia.' It forces him 'to look into the mirror and see someone else' and 'to deal creatively with one's own displaced condition.'[16] Similar to Kristeva, Sennett concludes by conflating the foreigner with the artist:

> And in this effort to displace the imagery of culture and folkways, the foreigner is engaged in a work akin to that of the modern artist whose energies have, in the last century, been marshalled not so much to represent objects, as to displace them.[17]

The similarities between the role and experience of the artist and those of the migrant have been identified and discussed by both theoreticians and artists themselves. Cultural theorist Mieke Bal, for instance, introduced the concept of 'migratory aesthetics.' She defines the modifier 'migratory' as 'a quality of the world in which mobility is no longer the exception but the standard.' The aesthetic encounter between a work of art and its viewer or spec-tator becomes migratory when it takes 'the mobility of people as central in the contemporary world.' She also defines 'globalized art' not as 'an art from nowhere' because all art is material and thus linked to a specific place and time, but as an artistic practice that 'addresses globalization as a problematic.'[18] It is my conviction that the productions by Sidi Larbi Cherkaoui and Akram Khan that I will discuss in chapter three fulfil the criteria to be called both 'migratory' and 'globalized' works of art. In what follows I will use the term 'migrating' rather than 'migratory' body, stressing less the qualitative aspect (as in a particular type of body) than the fact that this body is engaged in a continuous movement or oscillation.

But we also have to be careful not to overuse 'the metaphorization of migration.' Quoting amongst others Paul Carter's *Living in a New Country: History, Travelling and Language* (1992), Graham Huggan warns against this in 'Unsettled Settlers: Postcolonialism, Travelling Theory and the New Migrant Aesthetics,' his contribution to the collection *Essays in Migratory Aesthetics: Cultural Practices Between Migration and Art-making* (2007). He discusses how, following pioneers such as Edward Said and James Clifford, it became fashionable in cultural theory to use migration as a metaphor for both 'metaphysical and physical displacements,' such as 'the increasing fragmentation of the subject in (post)-modern thought' or 'the instability underlying all constructions of (personal, cultural, national) identity.'[19] He warns that this 'travelling theory' might overlook the reality and fundamental inequality between different migrant groups, for instance between those who are forced to migrate for political or economic reasons, and those, like myself, who have the freedom of choice to do so and go from one relatively stable context to another.

Rosi Braidotti, too, warns against 'superficial metaphorizations' which, she argues in 'Nomadic European Identity' (2015), can be prevented by embedding 'the different narratives in specific histories and geographies.'[20] Her overview and analysis of the current challenges facing Europe combine a realistic vision of the past and present with concrete utopian proposals for the future. Europe has to let go of its Eurocentric superiority and acknowledge that it is just 'one of the many peripheries in the world today':[21]

> The immediate consequence of the process of re-grounding European identity is that this hegemonic dialectical mode is undone in favour of multi-situated or 'nomadic' perspectives. The centre has to undergo a process of

becoming-other, becoming-minoritarian: being a nomadic European subject means to be in transit between different identity formations, but, at the same time, being sufficiently anchored to a historical position to accept responsibility for it.[22]

This necessary 'consciousness-raising' process that Europe has to engage with will not be easy or painless. It involves amongst other things a 'post-nationalist sense of European identity and of flexible citizenship' which requires leaving 'home' and 'changing deeply embedded habits, also in terms of imaginary self-representation.'[23] For the latter Braidotti sees a particular role for contemporary media and the cultural sector. Migrants have already gone through this process out of necessity and as such they might turn out to be ideal guides for the community as a whole. Braidotti repeats Homi K. Bhabha's appeal that 'a transnational, "migrant" knowledge of the world is most urgently needed.'[24]

In 2010, I decide for professional reasons to return to Europe and have since been living exactly the kind of post-nationalist, nomadic European identity that Braidotti describes. Stephanie Cumming, my wife, who is a Canadian performer and choreographer, and I are living in Vienna where 'home' is. We married in Montreal and I am still officially registered in Belgium where I pay my taxes. We both travel a lot for work and in order to write this book during a residence in Berlin, I also had to register there. Being flexible to live and work in several European countries at the same time also involves the acceptance of a certain precariousness regarding working and social conditions. And since I lost my status of permanent resident in Canada (for which you need to prove that you have resided on actual Canadian soil for a sufficient length of time), I am checked twice and questioned every time I travel back there. It is also getting harder to get a temporary work permit. My nomadic identity is constantly monitored, and from time to time restrictions to its mobility are imposed.

I began this first chapter with my own (hi)story, which I fully realize remains a rather privileged and relatively painless one compared to for instance the situation of the Syrian refugees. I did allow myself to start with my own autobiographical experience of migration in order to prevent a 'superficial metaphorization' of the term *migrant*, and to embed it in my own concrete narrative. In the next chapter I continue to explore the migrating identity with a focus on how Sidi Larbi Cherkaoui and Akram Khan both problematize and creatively use theirs in order to create and stimulate some of the 'lacking social imaginary [*sic*] that adequately reflects the social realities, which we are already experiencing, of a post-nationalist sense of nomadic European identity.'[25]

Notes

1   Keleman 1999, p. 76.
2   This first part was originally written for the program brochure of the symposium *Territoires en Mouvance* (2003). It was rewritten and expanded in Flemish for the book *Dans in Québec* (2008), with the title 'Nomadism as Point of Anchorage.'
3   Rushdie 2003, p. 408.
4   In his contribution to the *Granta* issue *New Europe*, Enzensberger writes an ode to the 'heroes who withdrew' and by doing so helped the dismantling of communism and dictatorship in Europe. He predicts that in the near future we will need to withdraw as well 'from our untenable position in the war of debt against the Third World,' and retreat 'in the war against the biosphere which we have been waging since the industrial revolution.' Enzensberger 1990, p. 142.
5   Rushdie 2003, p. 434.
6   Vooruit in Flemish actually means 'forward,' originally referring to the socialist avant-garde of the early twentieth century.
7   'Whatever the tense used, all utterance is a present act.' (Steiner 1975, p. 140) Inspired by this quote from George Steiner's *After Babel*, I permit myself to use all through this book mainly the present tense even when I am discussing the past as in my own, Sidi Larbi Cherkaoui's or Akram Khan's biographies.
8   Kristeva 1991, pp. 8–9.
9   For this they both refer to Nabokov as their exemplary model.
10   Rushdie 2002, p. 434.
11   Rushdie 1988, p. 427.
12   Kristeva 1991, p. 30.
13   I use 'somatic' in this book in a general and generative sense that is 'as related to the soma, the body.' How awareness, knowledge, and eventually also a sense of Self and identity are also generated on the level of the body. Dancers have a privileged access to this somatic awareness and knowledge and specific somatic practices have been developed to further stimulate it. In my own case, it has been a form of hatha yoga.
14   Chambers 1994, p. 27.
15   Sennett 2011, p. 58.
16   Ibid., p. 69.
17   Ibid., p. 92.
18   Bal 2007, pp. 23–26.
19   Huggan 2007, p. 131.
20   Braidotti 2015, p. 102.
21   Ibid., p. 94.
22   Ibid., p. 105.
23   Ibid., p. 110.
24   Bhabha 1994, p. 306.
25   Braidotti 2015, p. 108.

On a Migrating Identity

The academic debate within cultural studies on the importance and relevance of the notion of identity has been waxing and waning in the last few decades. But as dance scholar Ramsay Burt rightfully states, to speak of 'this decline of identity politics of the 1970s and 1980s is not to say that identity itself ceased to be an issue.'[1] In daily life questions of identity are still omnipresent. While I am writing this book as part of a residency at the Institute of Interweaving Performance Cultures at the Freie Universität in Berlin, the newspaper headlines refer to it on a daily basis. Like for instance today's: a page-long article in the *Berliner Zeitung* about a female German Muslim, with the title: 'My headscarf is Muslim but I am German,' and under her photo, the citation, 'But I still am who I am.'[2] In my own practice as a dance dramaturge, having worked with several generations of artists on different continents, I have noticed that the identity issue—whether of gender, race, culture, or religion—is still at the core of many artistic quests and a major source for many creative practices.

The relevance of both a critical reflection on the 'migrating body,' and an arts practice resulting from it, has recently been further highlighted by the project *Migrant Bodies* (2013–2015), which is supported by the EU Culture Programme. *Migrant Bodies* brings together artists from three different European countries (Croatia, France, and Italy) and two Canadian provinces (British Columbia and Quebec) 'to carry out two years of research on migrations and the social and cultural impacts that migrations generate in local societies in order to produce works of art.'[3] The results of the project are presented amongst others at the international meeting of the Association of European Cities and Region for Culture (Fontenay-sous-Bois, France, in the spring of 2015), whose main target group are European policymakers at the municipal level. By creating and presenting their work, the artists want to critically question 'the dominant codes and mainstream images,' collect new insights, and stimulate a new social imagery on the topic of migration.

Susanne Franco and Marina Nordera, in their edited volume *Dance Discourses: Keywords in Dance Research* (2007), list 'identity,' together with 'politics' and 'feminine/masculine,' as the keywords of actual dance research 'on basis of the frequency with which they appear in recent studies both inside and outside of the discipline.'[4] In 'Dance, Identity, and Identification Processes in the Postcolonial World,' Andrée Grau's 'state of the art'-section of the book, she observes that 'ours is a time of "post-identity" and that researchers engaged with identity are, in some circles, rather passé.' She concludes her contribution by reclaiming 'identity and alterity as pertinent concepts to understand the world we live in as well as imagine other worlds.'[5]

In this chapter I want to summarize some of the main voices and tendencies within the critical discourse on identity (as well as some that maybe haven't received so much attention). I also want to describe and analyze how Sidi Larbi Cherkaoui and Akram Khan, the two protagonists of this book, have related to and integrated some of these voices and ideas into their own formative discourse as artists. A lot of the existing discourse on cultural identity, such as for instance Homi K. Bhabha's notion of 'hybridity,' remains language-based, using as its mains sources literary texts. In discussing the work of choreographers such as Sidi Larbi Cherkaoui and Akram Khan, I want to show that the notion of identity is as much shaped by somatic experience as by language.

The Dominance of the Western, (Post)Modern Vision of Identity

It is by now common to assert that the centrality of the concept of identity in both theoretical and political discourses is a modern development.[6]

Stuart Hall, in his essay 'Who Needs "Identity"?' which introduces *Questions of Cultural Identity* (1996),[7] describes how the notion of identity in Western cultural theory shifted in the second half of the twentieth century from an essentialist discourse on 'integral, originary and unified identity.'[8] The critical discourse of thinkers such as Jacques Lacan, Jacques Derrida, Michel Foucault, and Judith Butler introduced a concept of identity 'under erasure,' which accepts 'that identities are never unified and, in late modern times, increasingly fragmented and fractured; never singular but multiply constructed across different, often intersecting and antagonistic, discourses, practices and positions.' Identities also arise from the fictionalization and 'narrativization of the Self.' They emerge 'within the play of specific modalities of power, marking difference and exclusion.'[9]

Most contributors to *Questions of Cultural Identity* criticize the dominance of the Western modern and postmodern view on culture and cultural identity, which divides neatly into the dichotomy of an essentialist, unifying concept of identity versus a more fragmented, open vision. In Zygmunt Bauman's essay in the book, 'From Pilgrim to Tourist–or a Short History of Identity,' the sociologist opposes the modernist vision–what he calls 'the problem of identity which was how to construct an identity and keep it solid and stable'–to the postmodern one which is 'primarily how to avoid fixation and keep the options open.'[10] He uses the figure of the pilgrim and its contemporary equivalents (such as the flâneur, the vagabond, the tourist, or the player) as exemplary figures to illustrate this condition. Marilyn Strathern, in her contribution, 'Enabling Identity? Biology, Choice and the New Reproductive Technologies,' states that Euro-Americans both invented modernity and 'reinvented tradition as pre-modern,' since modernity has always defined itself through differentiation from 'traditional societies.'[11] The latter argument is repeated by Kevin Robins in 'Interrupting Identities: Turkey/Europe.' Quoting Agnes Heller, he describes how 'modernity asserts itself through negation,' how it disturbingly 'defined itself against the pre-modern,' and how this polarity was translated geographically into the image of 'the dynamic West distinguishing itself from the static and immobile Orient.'[12] Meanwhile modernity has itself become Europe's tradition, 'to be remembered and revered' with little or no space 'for revision or reinvention.' Citing Georges Crom, Robins asserts that the history of this modernity is 'a narcissistic one,' focusing on the 'continuity of the Judaeo-Christian and Graeco-Roman heritage' and 'expelling any other influences (particularly Western Islam) from its collective memory.'[13]

Lawrence Grossberg, in his contribution 'Identity and Cultural Studies: Is that all there is?,' accurately summarizes the debate and gives a clear overview of the different positions within it. Following Hall, he distinguishes 'two models of production of identities.' The first model is based on the assumption that there is 'an intrinsic and essential content to any identity based on either a common origin or a common structure of experience.' The second rejects this essentialism of the first and instead defines identities as 'always relational and incomplete, in process,' depending 'upon their difference from, their negation of some Other.'[14] This second model, which remains the more accepted one today, is further defined and differentiated through a number of other figures and terms such as 'différance,' 'fragmentation,' 'diaspora,' and 'hybridity.' In différance, the negated and subordinate Other is an unnamable but constitutive element of the dominant culture's identity. Fragmentation focuses on the 'multiplicity' of identities. Diaspora links identity 'to spatial location and identifications.' Hybridity focuses on 'border existences' and is related to other images such as 'third space,' 'liminality,' and 'border crossing.' Grossberg also reiterates the argument that 'the "modern" constitutes its own identity by always differentiating itself from another, usually from tradition as a temporal other.'[15]

Introducing the notion of 'hybridity' and initiating the discourse that has been developed around it, Bhabha has taken a dominant place in the discussion of identity. In his contribution to *Questions of Cultural Identity?*, 'Culture's In-Between,' he criticizes Charles Taylor's liberal view of multiculturalism for being too optimistic and too homogenizing, turning 'the presumption of equality into the judgment of worth.'[16] Building on Mikhail Bakhtin's notion of the dialogic and the hybrid, Bhabha develops his own concept of hybridity in order 'to describe the construction of cultural authority within conditions of political antagonism or inequity.' According to him, a 'hybrid strategy or discourse opens up a space of negotiation' which is 'neither assimilation nor collaboration' but gives 'narrative form to the minority positions these identities occupy.'[17] Bhabha's concept of hybridity is thus a way of questioning and subverting cultural authority and as such is related to other notions, such as the 'in-between' and 'third space':

> To that end we should remember that it is the 'inter'—the cutting edge of translation and negotiation, the inbetween space—that carries the burden of meaning of culture. [...] And by exploring this Third Space, we may elude the politics of polarity and emerge as the others of our selves.[18]

Bhabha has always made it very clear that his concepts of hybridity and Third Space have been developed within the specific context of (post)colonial power relations, which is why he rejects their application to the discussion of mere identity construction.[19] His multilayered reflections are themselves an example of the borderline experience of postmodern writing. Using as their primary sources and points of reference literary texts, they discuss the formation and problems of cultural identity primarily in and through language, 'learning to work with the contradictory strains of languages lived, and languages learned.'[20] In what follows I will therefore draw on other authors, such as for example Daniel Sibony, who has applied his notion of the 'in-between' to dance.

Bhabha also warns about the ongoing 'disproportionate influence of the West as the cultural forum, that is, as a place of exhibition and discussion, a place of judgment and as market place.'[21] I, too, feel that in certain circles, not necessarily among artists but among certain opinion makers such as critics and curators, there has recently been an attempt at 'restoration' of the Western modernist worldview, not only in political discourses but also in the discourse around the arts. Ignoring the geopolitical changes and the paradigm shifts that mark the beginning of the twenty-first century, they try to reinstall a hierarchy between high and popular art, valuing highest the traditional Western modernist ideals of 'purity' of form and 'originality,' which they see as standing at the top of the pyramid. This also seems to be the case in the recent phenomenon of museums of contemporary art embracing dance, as their focus remains firmly on Western modern and postmodern dance forms and their more recent conceptual or self-reflexive variants. The latter robs dance also of its own unique history to art galleries (not museums).

Related to the above is also a need to revalorize some of these dominant, Western values which are used to 'judge' artistic value and identity. Twentieth-century Western art has been dominated by the concepts of 'originality' and 'innovation.' The nineteenth-century prelude to the romantic era introduces them. The modern era celebrates them. The postmodern age shows their relativism but doesn't question their value or ontological status. And our media-oriented consumer culture still defines them as two major assets and characteristics of the brand 'contemporary art.'

This stress on 'innovation' often feels like an accelerated, forced, and ultimately imposed quality of what is essentially an organic and slow process. It takes time to 'embody' new information and knowledge. Every creative act is in essence transformative in the way it translates a number of sources into a new work. When this process is accelerated, it runs the risk of becoming incomprehensible and therefore meaningless. In the introduction to the book *Creativity and Cultural Improvisation* (2007), edited by Elizabeth Hallam and Tim Ingold, the editors plead for a (re) valorization of the notion of 'improvisation,' in opposition to the more fashionable term of 'innovation.' According to Ingold, the use of the latter within the contemporary discourse on creativity remains stuck within a modernist paradigm that equals creativity with innovation and defines it as 'produced novelty,' that is, as a characteristic of a given end-product. Ingold proposes an alternative discourse that focuses on 'improvisation' which is generative in the way that it always deals with a 'growing emergence' and as such is a forward movement that stresses the 'becoming' of things:

> The difference between improvisation and innovation, then, is not that the one works within established convention while the other breaks with it, but that the former characterizes creativity by the way of its processes, the latter by the way of its products.[22]

The concept of 'originality' is even more problematic because it denies all influences and pretends that the creative act is its own origin. It implies that one is able to create 'out of the blue,' relating only to the present moment and, having no history, being self-sufficient without sources or influences. As such it denies all individual and collective histories that manifest themselves as permanent states of transition, infinite chains of influences and shifts.

Choreographers such as Sidi Larbi Cherkaoui and Akram Khan belong to a different generation, one that looks to reconcile all its influences. 'I privilege a relational dance in contact with the outside world, following up one's masters, in a continuation of tradition. My art is first and foremost a dialogue, a continuation.'[23] In what follows I want to describe how Sidi Larbi Cherkaoui and Akram Khan develop a discourse around their artistic work for themselves, borrowing from the above-described critical debate on 'cultural identity.' At the same time I will introduce a number of other voices in the debate, including Daniel Sibony on 'the in-between,' Amin Malouf on 'multiple identities' and Stanley Keleman on 'myth and the body.'

The Ambivalent Nature of the (Post-)Migrant Identity

> Cherkaoui's appointment sends an important signal. He is the first Belgian with foreign roots—his father is Moroccan, his mother Flemish—to lead one of Flanders' major cultural institutions.[24]

In the beginning of February 2015, the Royal Ballet of Flanders announces that they appointed Sidi Larbi Cherkaoui as their new artistic director. The ballet company has been going through an artistic identity crisis for several years. They have been looking for a new balance between on the one hand the balletic heritage that they have been preserving and defending, and on the other a sense of relevance within a contemporary Flemish dance field that, since the early 1980s, has been completely renewed by a generation of internationally acclaimed choreographers such as Anne Teresa De Keersmaeker, Alain Platel, or Wim Vandekeybus. Sidi Larbi Cherkaoui might be the ideal person to bridge both worlds, having a strong foot in each: he is one of the most successful international contemporary choreographers of his generation and has also created works for major ballet companies including amongst others the Stuttgart Ballet, Paris Opera Ballet, Cullberg Ballet, Les Ballets de Monte-Carlo, and the Dutch National Ballet. However, as the quote above shows, the media coverage that follows the press announcement not only focuses on his artistic merits but also on his identity as a second-generation migrant.

Since 2012, Sidi Larbi Cherkaoui has a monthly column in the progressive Flemish Internet magazine *MO*,[25] an acronym for *Mondiaal Nieuws* [World News]. The magazine is a media platform for a number of NGOs in Belgium such as Oxfam, 11.11.11, and Fairtrade Belgium. One of its goals is to increase awareness of and inform on sustainable development in the Southern Hemisphere, as well as report on (other forms of) globalization. In his monthly column Larbi reflects on world news with a preference for the topics that concern him personally, such as gay rights, healthy (vegan) food, the importance of the arts, religious tolerance, and cultural diversity. On his global travels he writes about the places he is working in, for example gambling madness in Los Angeles when working for Cirque du Soleil, being in the eye of Hurricane Sandy in New York, or in Japan at the time of the Fukushima disaster. Another recurrent theme in his columns is his (self-)reflection on the ambivalent and problematic nature of his (post-)migrant identity.

One entry for his columns bears the title 'One surname, a lot of future.' In it, Sidi Larbi Cherkaoui considers his recent nomination as one of the twenty-five most influential migrants in Belgium in one of the annual polls that are published at the end of each year. 'Migrant literally means coming from another country, in which case I should have been disqualified in the poll,' he reflects, 'since I was born here. My father, who migrated from Tangiers, Morocco, could have been nominated. But it seems the word "migrant" is transferable. It also sticks to your children.' He continues to describe his ancestry on his mother's side which is a very Flemish identity rooted in a working class environment. 'Epic stories about child labor, families with 13 children, deadly diseases and unexpected deaths which in Flanders seem to belong to the past but which in other parts of the world are still a present day reality.' He also reflects on how the label of migrant is only selectively used for certain ethnic backgrounds, recognizable by their name. If you are white and have a Western background, you are called an expat or not labeled at all. He concludes that it is not his mixed roots which define him as (post-)migrant but his name, and he pleads for an approach that recognizes the complementarity of the different aspects of his identity. 'It is not one or the other, but both, migrant and Flemish and from Antwerp, speaking with the local accent that is very recognizable. A surname is a label that clarifies your roots, but it shouldn't determine your present or your future.'[26]

Sidi Larbi Cherkaoui is not the only artist reflecting on his own name and how it influences the way he is perceived. The Congolese choreographer Faustin Linyekula defines his dance as 'an attempt to remember his name' and to create from his name 'a web of relationships to people and places.' He describes how his first name was given to him in correspondence with his uncle, the twin brother of his father, and how this uncle received his name as part of a Christian baptizing campaign that was introduced during the colonial period in a similar way as last names. He also discusses how Mobutu, in an attempt to erase the colonial past, introduced another set of names, 'post names' and forbade people to use their 'original' names at risk of prison penalty. Faustin concludes that researching his name is a life-long artistic journey and an attempt to understand himself.[27]

Another major discussion in the debate on (post-)migrant identity has to do with whether this identity is primarily defined in spatial terms of geographical displacement or in temporal terms of having to negotiate different 'traditions,' which Bhabha defines as 'the non-synchronous temporality of global and national cultures opening up a cultural space—a third space.'[28] In my own reflections and writing I have often replaced the intercultural with the 'bi- or multi-temporal,' where the negotiation between different cultures and identities is mainly one between different time experiences. For instance Akram Khan describes how as a child he constantly had to negotiate between the time at school with his peers coming from a variety of cultural backgrounds but sharing an interest in the same music (Michael Jackson) and the same film heroes (Bruce Lee) and the time at home with the daily rituals, the food and the cultural affinities of his family. As both Bhabha's characterization of Third Space and Akram's example illustrate, spatial and temporal experiences are always interrelated and hard to separate.

In another column in March 2014, Sidi Larbi Cherkaoui quotes the Nigerian author Chimamanda Ngozi Adichie, who writes that 'denying the reality of race is a white privilege.' He describes his own ambiguous feelings growing up as 'an undercover Arab' with white skin and speaking the local dialect, but with an Arab heritage and surname. 'Your behavior is changed by the way your environment looks at you and treats you. [...] Racism is more than disrespect for the otherness of people; it sticks a psychological imprint on the other which actually changes him.'[29] In order to escape any such categorization, Sidi Larbi Cherkaoui systematically defines his own identity as an identity 'in-between.'

A Liminal Identity In-between

> Maybe the challenges of the in-between lead to movements, more or less rich, where an identity tries to recollect its fragments, to integrate itself (while believing it is integrating with others), to assume oneself as a clown's outfit in the circus of the world.[30]

Homi K. Bhabha's notions of hybridity, 'third space,' and liminality resemble the concept of the 'in-between' described by French philosopher and psychiatrist Daniel Sibony. In his book, *Entre-deux: l'origine en partage* (1991), Sibony defines identity as a 'movement in-between,' 'an open process' in which one has to integrate the 'stranger' and 'the event of otherness as well as oneself.'[31] He distinguishes between the 'in-between' and the notion of 'difference.' Difference always describes a simplistic polarity between the sexes, between religions and cultures, between life and death, between have and have-nots, between good and bad. It implies a static division, marked by a borderline and symbolized by a trait. 'The idea of a border or trait, with an inside and outside, a here and a there seems insufficient.' The in-between, on the other hand, is both a space and a movement, a dynamic and often instable oscillation—'It defines a vast space where reattachments and integrations should be flexible, mobile and rich in games of differentiation.'[32] When an identity crisis arises, it is thus a problem of the in-between, that is, a difficulty in accepting the constant oscillation between the different polarities. 'Our identity is a pulsation which prevents us to identify completely with one pole and it renews itself constantly in the passageway from one to the other.'[33] As Lin Snelling remarked when proofreading the manuscript of this book, the latter resembles the very processes of our own breathing.

Sibony's notion of the in-between is related to the notion of a shared but unstable 'origin.' For Sibony our origins are not fixed points in time or space but always impure and contaminated points of departure, shared with others, only there to be left and to be lost.[34] It is when one gets stuck in a false idea of a pure origin, which we only remember in a fragmentary and stereotypical way, that the danger of fanaticism lurks.

Not by coincidence, Sibony's book begins with a chapter on the 'stranger' and the 'migrant,' and concludes with another on 'travelling.' Sibony, who is himself of mixed Arabic, Jewish, and French origin, describes many cases of migrant children growing up in-between languages and cultures. He also underlines that their situation is less unique than we suppose. We all grow up in-between the presence or absence of both our parents and the lineages that they bring with them. 'In a family there are always at least two languages: the language of the father and the language of the mother, an internal and a cultural language, an esoteric language, the language of tradition, the language of family dreams.'[35] In growing up the child has to learn and to dare to interpret and translate these languages in order to create his or her own identity.

Echoing how Sidi Larbi Cherkaoui describes both his attachment to his birthplace, Antwerp, and his need to travel [in the ARTE documentary *Dreams of Babel* (2010)], Sibony discusses how 'places as fragments of our identity are precarious points of anchorage in an origin, which is nothing less than a point of departure of being.'[36] Recalling Bauman's notion of the pilgrim, Sibony writes that 'the idea of travelling is not about the way, but the desire of wayfaring, to let oneself and the here be seduced by a there, to move in-between and to displace oneself.'[37] Tim Ingold, too, uses the image of the 'wayfarer'—someone who is continually on the move, who 'is his movement' and who gathers his knowledge on his 'journey through the world along paths of travel' as 'a knot of stories.'[38]

In the discourse they have developed to describe their creative practice and its sources, both Akram Khan and Sidi Larbi Cherkaoui explicitly refer to and identify themselves as growing up in-between two parental influences. Akram identifies the pole of his 'classical' Kathak work with his father, and his contemporary work with his mother:

> My classical work [...] relates very much to my father and my father's body—because growing up in front of my father's eyes there was something very classical about him. There was a huge amount of form around him. There were rules, there were regulations. Everything was almost mathematical with my father; he is an accountant, so it does not surprise. But there was a very strict relationship with him, and that comes from his own personal experience. He grew up in a family where he was the head; he had to run his family because his father lost his job and so on. So there was some kind of authority about him. He built all these walls and rules and they were very precise, and so, in the way my father stands... when he turns his head the whole body turns. And his whole way of expressing himself, of course I was picking this up as a child—so in my classical work I relate to him.
>
> And then there is the company work which I would say is much more my mother. With my mother's body everything is more circular; it is more huggable if you like, and there is something exactly the opposite of my father's— very formless, very creative. She was a folk dancer; but she adapted, because her father did not allow her to dance. She would secretly go and learn classical dance, and when she wasn't allowed to do classical dance she would do pop dance, or she would do something else. She was constantly reinventing herself to survive, to stay connected to the arts in Bangladesh at a time when she was not allowed to, and so her body language is much more circular, much softer. That influence—her body's influence—comes into my contemporary work.[39]

In her feminist reading of *Pichet Klunchun and Myself* (2004), the artistic collaboration between the French choreographer Jérôme Bel and the Thai dancer Pichet Klunchun, Susan Leigh Foster analyzes how in that work, the gender categories of male and female are associated with the binary terms contemporary and traditional in the opposite way from Akram Khan. 'In this dyad the feminine is fleshed out through its association with tradition, unquestioning allegiance to social order, [...] In contrast, the masculine is embodied as experimental and contemporary; as always questioning, conducting research, presenting the latest reality.'[40] *Pichet Klunchun and Myself* remains a typical Western, postmodern, and conceptual work that stereotypically confirms the old hierarchies between male and female, West and East.

In an interview Sidi Larbi Cherkaoui defines himself as 'a metis who at a young age understood that he didn't belong to any clan,' adding 'that everybody comes from at least two family lineages and possesses at least a double identity.'[41] In a similar way in the film *Dreams of Babel* (2009), he discusses his being part of a triangle in-between his mother and father: 'A triangle that shaped my way of thinking, my behavior, my flaws and my qualities.' He describes how his father never accepted him, his homosexuality, his wanting to pursue a career as a dancer. 'I felt like a secondhand son.' Only after his parents' divorce, when he is fifteen years old, can he fully begin to realize his own dreams.

He also describes how much he wanted to be like other children, but how his Arabic name made him different and obliged him to explain who he was and where he came from all the time. Larbi literally means 'the Arab' while Cherkaoui means 'coming from the East.' Early on in his career he would develop a preference for working in Asia, whether in China (for *Sutra*, 2008), India (for *Play*, 2010), or Japan (amongst others *TeZukA*, 2011). It is in Asia that he feels more at home, connected through his name and his ancestors. When he finally creates his own company in 2010, he appropriately calls it 'Eastman.' The ARTE documentary shows Larbi either in his hometown Antwerp, wandering along the streets or the river, or has him travelling on different means of transport to the global places at which he works: Chennai, India; Lumio, Corsica; or the Shaolin Monastery in Henan, China. His identity seems to be rooted in the voyage and he remembers the annual summer car journey to Morocco as a ritual initiation in different stages, with the boat passage to Tangiers as its final stage of 'arriving.' 'I multiply my travels, without being a tourist. Each meeting changes me forever. Each transformation encourages me to continue to change. To move. It is without doubt the place where I feel most at ease to work, to transform, to feel free: at the margin or in transit.'[42]

Where for Akram Khan the in-between his two parents is culturally more homogenous and rooted, for Sidi Larbi Cherkaoui it also represents the in-between of cultures and religions: Western European and catholic versus North African and Muslim. From his early work onward, he identifies certain creations more with one pole or the other. *Foi* (2003) is about his Western European and Catholic roots, while a piece like *Tempus Fugit* (2004), which follows it, expresses his Arabic sensitivity: 'When I explore the Arabic culture in *Tempus Fugit*, I want to show it as an in-between link between North African and Southern European cultures. In the same way that I am a link between my mother and my father, half-Belgian and half-Moroccan. And these two cultures have a lot in common, because I exist and bring them together.'[43]

Philosopher Liesbeth Levy characterizes this situation of growing up in-between the two cultures represented by both parents as a doublebind. Discussing the work of the French-Gabonese visual artist Myriam Mihindou, she describes how growing up as the child of a so-called domino couple requires negotiating the doublebind, which she defines as 'a dilemma in communication in which an individual receives two contradictory messages' at two different levels: 'in the outer world between minority and majority' and 'in the intimate space of your own family.'[44]

Sibony is a dance aficionado as well as a philosopher and psychoanalyst. In his book *Le corps et sa danse* (1995), he uses his notion of the in-between to offer one of the most pertinent definitions of dance. He defines dance as a movement in-between two bodies: a *corps-mémoire* [body-memory] and a *corps actuel* [body-present]. The passageway from one to the other, which always takes place in both directions at the same time, is both an act of *appel* [calling out] to the present and *rappel* [recalling] the past.[45] It is easy to see how this definition, which is both very simple and highly complex, can be applied to different aspects of the creative process and performative practice. In every dance or theatre tradition, the training and technique of the dancers is there to establish meaningful links between the memory of the body and its presence. *bahok* (2008) by Akram Khan, which I discuss in detail in the next chapter gives concrete examples of how the dancers' memories about their childhood homes are used to generate both narratives and movements. Different 'schools' often define themselves in the way they stress one more than the other or try to establish this 'link' through different approaches (for instance a psychological one versus a more formal one). Every creative rehearsal process aims at finding a balance between the unique 'appeal' of the creative act, the possibility of repeating it and recreating it an infinite number of times, and giving to the presentation of this act of remembering the quality and presence of the original.

Every dance performance thus recreates its creation in front of an audience. The time and space of the performance need to balance the deep structure of the rehearsal practice with the surface structure of the actual performance in a unique way. The movement the dancer makes between his body-memory and his present body is an 'appeal' to the spectator to do the same, that is, by viewing or sensing the present-a(c)tion to remember its past, its origin, its meaning. Ideally the corporeal memories of the dancer trigger the memories of the spectator without them having to be identical or coincide.

What is true for the individual dancer, spectator, or performance, is also true for the history of dance (or any other art form). It reads as a movement between 'a body of memories'—a tradition—and the re-actualization of this body in the con-temporary, that is, a 'being with the time' and a 'being present.' 'Traditional' and 'contemporary' as such should not be considered as opposing qualifications but as integral, complementary parts of any creative process.

In *The Six Seasons* (2012), the film documentary on the creation process of *Desh* (2011), Akram Khan talks about his own experience as a dancer in a way that recalls Sibony's definition of dance. He explains how being in the present is the most 'truthful moment,' and how he has 'to tap into his memory to force the body to react to that memory.'[46]

In chapter 3, I describe in more detail a number of creations by Sidi Larbi Cherkaoui and Akram Khan in which they consciously use the 'body-memory' of their identity 'in-between' cultures to question our habits and trigger a new social imagery.

A Multiple, Polyphonic Identity

> The polyphony of being: that is my obsession, if you like, and this is as much philosophical as aesthetical.[47]

Dreams of Babel (2009) begins with a quote in which Sidi Larbi Cherkaoui describes his multiple identity:

> I am a man. I am a son, a choreographer. I am Belgian, homosexual. I have a tattoo, brown eyes. I am the son of an immigrant. My name is Sidi Larbi Cherkaoui.

It resonates with the ideas that Lebanese author Amin Malouf develops in his book *Les identités meurtrières* [In the Name of Identity] (1998), about how we all have multiple or composite identities which are situational, changing with time and depending on the context we are in. I am a different person at home with family than I am with my friends or at work. Each time I highlight different aspects of my identity. Each of these aspects (being male or female, having a particular nationality or religion, having a certain profession) links me with another group of people and it is the combination of all these individual aspects that builds my own, unique personality.[48] The different aspects of my identity often have a hierarchy amongst each other which changes with time and due to external circumstances. Andrée Grau also cites Malouf and defines identity as 'dialogic' in the way that it is 'constructed through dialogue with the other,' constantly soliciting 'principles of affiliation and differentiation.'[49] She transposes Malouf's idea of the individual or the community to cultural artifacts. To Malouf's example of the shifting identity of an inhabitant of the Balkans in recent history, she adds the example of the Ganga music of the same region, which from 'symbolizing a rural and mountain identity that was capable of transcending religion and ethnicity' became re-identified with a nationalist agenda during the conflicts of the late 1980s.

Malouf describes how all these aspects of our identity are interconnected, causing the entirety to vibrate when one of them is touched. 'The identity of a person is not a juxtaposition of autonomous aspects; it is not a "patchwork," it is a drawing on a tight skin. If you touch one aspect, it is the whole person that vibrates.'[50] In a similar way Larbi describes in the ARTE documentary how he felt that specific parts of his identity, like for example being Arab, or homosexual, challenged all the others. Malouf also distinguishes two directionalities of our multiple identity: a horizontal one defined through 'one's time and peers,' through our own life choices—the career we choose, the friends we make both in daily life and on Facebook, the way we fashion ourselves—and a vertical one which is determined by our heritage, including notions such as race, nation, and religion. In the twenty-first century the horizontal dimension seems to have become the more important one. However, the vertical one often tries to pull us back in.

It is this vertical identity that is at the core of most conflicts, both for the individual and in society, hence Malouf's title 'deadly identities.' Certain aspects of our own identity such as religion, ethnicity, or nationality become deadly when they claim to be the essential one and when they take over the whole identity, suppressing all the other aspects. On the other hand, people who live at the borderlines or the fractures of different aspects of their identity, migrants, for example, have the potential to be bridge-builders between the different communities and cultures they are part of, on the condition that they fully embrace and can live 'the diversity of their identity.' Increasingly, this state of having to live on the frontiers of our identity is no longer unique to the migrant, but is a state we all experience in a globalized world.

Malouf continues to unfold this problematic, giving examples from different places in the world that have dominated the news in the past decades: the Middle East, the Balkans, the African continent. Situating them in the context of both the dominance and the crisis of Western modernity, he evaluates the opportunities and challenges of the global availability of new information and communication technologies. Globalization creates 'a movement towards two opposing realities: universalism and uniformity.'[51] According to Malouf, we have to embrace the first and avoid the latter by celebrating both the diversity of languages and cultures and their reciprocity and exchange. 'Between the language we identify with and the global language, there is a vast space, an immense space that one should learn to fill.'[52] We can reach out to other cultures by genuinely learning their languages. This is exactly the task Sidi Larbi Cherkaoui has set out for himself within the dance world.

Sidi Larbi Cherkaoui explicitly refers to Malouf and his ideas on multiple identities when he gives the 'State of the Union' address at the Theaterfestival in 2008. The Theaterfestival is a yearly reunion of the Dutch and Flemish performing arts community, centring around a selection of the most remarkable performances of the past season. In Flanders it is introduced by the 'State of the Union' address, in which an artist from the community expresses concerns about the state of the art and his or her vision for its future. In his 'State of the Union,' Sidi Larbi Cherkaoui describes ten dreams for a future theatre landscape. He transfers Malouf's notion of multiple identities from the individual (himself) to the whole of the contemporary Flemish theatre landscape. 'Contemporary also involves the past and traditional. Flemish involves international and multicultural. Theatre needs to be connected with dance, music, literature and popular culture.'[53] He concludes his first dream by wishing for a theatre landscape that is 'totally inclusive' and includes all forms of expression from the popular and the traditional to the contemporary, none of which should exclude each other but coexist as complementary forms of one 'large social network.' To this first dream he adds others, wishing 'for a theatre without hierarchies,' 'for a theatre language that includes all other languages,' 'for a theatre genealogy that realizes that both its branches and its roots keep growing,' 'for a migrating theatre,' 'for a theatre without prejudices,' and 'for theatre as play.' He acknowledges that some of these dreams might be considered naïve and he humorously questions his public, Flemish identity. 'This year in Avignon, they talked again of the Flemish Theatre Wave, which I was considered being part of, with *Sutra*. The latter is made with seventeen Shaolin monks, a Polish composer, and a British stage designer. I think it would have been a very different work if I had used Flemish monks.'[54]

In the same 'State of the Union,' Sidi Larbi Cherkaoui also questions the modernist need to be 'original' and to deny one's sources and role models, and instead pleads for 'theatre as a mimetic learning process.' 'I wanted to copy my role models: Pina Bausch's movements, William Forsythe's mathematical insights or Alain Platel's social themes. Even when you copy, things transform and they become part of your own language.'[55] Transmission of knowledge happens through copying one's role models but also through the exchange and integration of each other's stories.

Identity as Storytelling

> I create who I am with the stories I tell. I write myself into
> existence by the stories that I tell about my life.[56]

Artists often create their own stories and myths to explain
the origins of their creative impulses and their desire to create.
A well-known example is Louise Bourgeois, who dedicated her
entire seventy-year long career as one of the twentieth century's
most influential visual artists to one childhood memory of her
father being unfaithful to her mother with her English governess.
In her own, recent autobiographical dance solo *Hunter* (2014)
Meg Stuart rightfully questions Bourgeois's fictionalization of her
own artistic identity and origin as an unnecessary understatement
of the immensity of the oeuvre resulting from it. But still, such
selective remembering of the stories of our past become constitutive parts of our identity. We all selectively remember parts of
our own history and biography (including those of our parents
and ancestors), which we tell over and over again to explain
ourselves to others. This act of remembering is always one of
deconstruction and transformation. Our memory is always subjective. Already in the moment of experiencing through the senses,
the memory takes apart factual experience and reassembles it by
stressing certain parts and forgetting others, by reordering them
according to a logic that seems appropriate and makes sense to the
self that remembers. In his contribution to the book *ReMembering
the Body* (2000), Jan Assmann discusses in detail the history and
symbolism of the 'membra disiecta': the rituals of embalmment
which place the body at the centre of the individual's biographical
memory bank. He sees the myth of Osiris, whose dismember-
ment and subsequent re-collection (that is, the collection of his
dispersed body parts and their reassembling by Isis), as a symbolic
representation of the collective cultural memory of a country
or community:

> This act of searching, collecting and assembling together
> [...] in which the Egyptians continuously assure themselves
> of the endangered identity and integrity of their culture—
> is something which one is compelled to link with the
> English concepts 're-collection' and 're-membering' [...]
> which, in their basic etymological meaning, signify nothing

other than 'collecting together again' and 'assembling together again.'[57]

In a similar way, Iain Chambers, in *Migrancy, Culture, Identity* (1994), draws a parallel between the way we construct our own individual narratives and the way the narrative of nations involves the construction of an 'imaginary community, a sense of belonging sustained as much by fantasy and the imagination as by any geographical or physical reality.'[58]

In the process of remembering and retelling, both the story and the identity resulting from it are transformed. In 'Stories against classification: transport, wayfaring and the integration of knowledge', a chapter in his book *Being Alive, Essays on Movement, Knowledge and Description* (2011), Tim Ingold discusses the acquisition and transmission of knowledge. He rejects a vertical, genealogical, and classificatory model where knowledge is given and inherited prior to experience. He proposes knowledge to be 'storied,' that is, to result from moving and travelling through the world and by doing so learning and understanding the relations between ourselves and our environment. Ingold's notion of 'storied' knowledge also revalorizes other forms of transmission and exchange, particularly oral and somatic ones, over the dominant written mode:

> To know someone or something is to know their story, and to be able to join that story to one's own. Yet, of course, people grow in knowledge not only through direct encounters with others, but also through hearing their stories told. To tell a story is to relate, in narrative, the occurrences of the past, bringing them to life in the vivid present of listeners as if they were going on here and now.[59]

What is true for knowledge is also true for our identity. We develop and transform our identity constantly by remembering and retelling our stories selectively, and by sharing them with others. Art is thus a particular form of storytelling that has an identity-(trans)forming capacity both for its creator and its recipient. In *What's the Story: Essays about Art, Theater and Storytelling* (2014) Anne Bogart discusses how the identity-forming quality of storytelling is related to the theatre experience. Quoting findings in neuroscience, she describes how stories 'engage the entire brain' and how they have 'the potential to make strong, visceral impressions, which in turn can transform attitudes, which then can alter behavior.'[60]

The last point has been further developed in important ways by Stanley Keleman and Joseph Campbell. From 1973 until 1987 (the year of Campbell's death), Stanley Keleman, pioneer in somatic therapy and Joseph Campbell, eminent scholar of Western mythology, organized a series of annual seminars to exchange their views of how mythology relates to and is expressed in the somatic processes of the body. *Myth & the Body: A colloquy with Joseph Campbell* by Keleman and published in 1999, is a transcription of parts of these taped seminars.

In their dialogues, Campbell and Keleman discuss how all myths are about the body itself. 'Myth is about the body's journey, recreating itself endlessly in a particular way, to form an individual, personal structure called self.'[61] If our DNA is our genetic code, 'myths are scripts of these genetic shapes in social language.' They tell stories of our coming into the world (birth), our departure (death) and all the stages of transformation in-between. They translate the changes of our metabolism into mythic images and metaphors such as the snake being the spinal column, or the cortex being reimagined as 'the thousand petals lotus' or 'the crown of thorns.' These stories always describe a journey, a path of embodiment. 'The function of myth is to put experience into stories, because stories are the organizers of bodily experience, of ways to form ourselves as individuals.'[62]

In *The Foreigner* (2011), Richard Sennett, too, gives a good example of the ways in which stories and myths are about the body. He uses the story of Oedipus, in particular the scars on his body, to discuss two conditions of the foreigner. One scar (his pierced ankle) references the importance of origins and of belonging, while the second, self-inflicted scar (the piercing of the eyes) marks him as an eternal wanderer and exile. 'The two scars on the body of King Oedipus represent a fundamental conflict in our civilization between the truth-claims of place and beginnings versus the truths to be discovered in becoming a foreigner.'[63]

I would like to add another story of my own to further illustrate Keleman's claim that our identity is always also somatically shaped, and that the stories which we tell often give expression to somatic experiences and transformations. When I am in my early forties, I begin to suffer regularly from lower back pain. Eventually, my osteopath diagnoses its origin in the difference in length between my two legs, my left leg being one-and-a-half centimeters longer than my right. As a result I distribute my weight unevenly and I also discover that while walking my right foot hardly touches ground—it is floating all the time. An elevation in the right shoe and a new consciousness of how to place both my feet down not only realign my whole body—the first days being an energetic rollercoaster—but also and more importantly gives me a new sense of being literally better grounded in my body through the newly apprehended contact of both my feet with the earth. Not being grounded enough has always been a key issue in my personal psychology and behaviour. My own story, Sennett's interpretation of the Oedipus myth and Campbell and Keleman's discussion of *Myth & the Body* are all examples of how we create narratives about the transformation of our somatic identity.

> Whether we like it or not, we are incarnated. We are bodies on this planet, and all myth and all stories seek the origin and the end of our somatic structure. Myth as story is the life of our body in one or another of its forms. We are all making up stories, finding stories, finding facts to talk about our somatic origin, its growth and its end.[64]

Artists, who are constantly challenged by the increased mediatization of their biography, are particularly good at the abovementioned way of storytelling that forms part of their own (artistic) identity. Sidi Larbi Cherkaoui and Akram Khan are no exception to this. One of Larbi's favourite stories is how his artistic interest and sensibility has been formed by his mother showing him the sculptures and paintings in the Cathedral of Our Lady in Antwerp. He has used this story to relativize the notion of artistic taste which is also culturally determined, explaining that some of his Eastern collaborators and guests didn't see any beauty in these cruel images of violence and death. He also uses it to defend himself against the opinion of certain critics that the imagery of his 'baroque' contemporary dance is too dense for an audience to grasp:

> I remember a journalist from Greece who had seen it (*Myth*) once and told me: 'I think it is too much.' He was in Antwerp, so I brought him to the cathedral there, to see the sculpture at the entrance, which is really huge and full

of apostles and all of that. You can't take it in, it is just too much. And I asked him: 'Do you think the artist is doing too much here?' He understood. When you really focus on the cathedral, you can see the story.[65]

Lise Uytterhoeven dedicates a whole chapter of her doctoral thesis, *New Dramaturgies in the Work of Sidi Larbi Cherkaoui* (2013), to 'the choreographer as storyteller.' She analyses how Sidi Larbi Cherkaoui 'addresses political and societal issues through the active discovery of the performers' cultural backgrounds, focusing on the transmission of cultural knowledge through oral and embodied practices' with a preference for travel stories and experiences of a performer 'with a destabilized sense of Self due to cultural mixedness or geographical displacement.'[66]

The Kathak dancer is in essence a storyteller (*kathaka* in Sankrit). As a result, Akram Khan, on stage as well as off, is a great creator of stories to explain and contextualize his work. One of his favourites is of him getting stuck in the elevator of a hotel while on tour in Japan. He describes how the lift fills with people from different nationalities—Japanese, African, European, and American—each dressed in their particular outfits. How these different people in close proximity first ignore each other, with 'lots of walls being created in such a tiny space.' And how the moment the lift gets stuck all these people start engaging with each other, talking to each other, 'how in a moment of crisis everybody comes together regardless of language, culture, or how you look.'[67]

Akram's story resonates with the ideas that Rebecca Solnit develops in her book *A Paradise Built in Hell: The Extraordinary Communities that Arise in Disaster* (2009). Solnit describes, with a lot of factual details and deep insights, how major disasters such as terrorist attacks or natural disasters bring out the best in people as shown in their immediate responses (her examples range from the Halifax Explosion of 1917 to 9/11 and Hurricane Katrina): spontaneous actions of self-organization, generosity, and solidarity across traditional divides of class or ethnicity.

The stories that Sidi Larbi Cherkaoui and Akram Khan create, both inside their artistic practice and in the discourse accompanying it, often focus on the different somatic polarities of their multiple identities in-between and how they creatively move between them.

> Fusion feels too much like perfection. It is a perfect thing, where two things fuse together to create something that becomes one. It is too much of a fantasy for me. I find it much more complex. [...] The sense of chaos in the body, or the confusion, seemed a word that was much more relevant to the state I was in then, and the state I am in, even more now.[68]

In his paper 'Contemporary Dance and the Performance of Multicultural Identities' (2004), Ramsay Burt argues that a choreographer such as Akram Khan is representative of a generation of artists whose work no longer relates to the host culture (contemporary Western art practices) in terms of accommodation or resistance, but really has the potential to contribute to and influence the host culture by creating 'an appreciation and openness towards difference.' Burt describes how so-called classical Indian dance has been revived in its home country in order to support a postcolonial national identity. Navtej Johar, in his essay 'The Power of Seeing' (2014), gives a similarly detailed account of how both yoga and bharatanatyam were 'cleansed' and 'domesticated' as part of a middle-class, Indian nationalistic agenda. In a second wave, these cultural expressions became a binding element for creating or maintaining a common identity in the dispersed communities of migrants all over the world, which Burt characterizes as a 'diasporic account which would stress continuities of practice across geographical boundaries.'[69] This is necessary in order to finally reach a stage where they can begin to interact with the host culture, creating 'the potential to suggest new possibilities of egalitarian co-existence': the 'hybrid account.' The critical reception of Akram Khan, from his early works onward, for example *Kaash* (2002), has shown how he is being both fully embraced as 'contemporary British,' and seen as being a part of 'dancing in the diaspora,' as evidenced by his inclusion in an overview of *Contemporary Indian Dance: New Creative Choreography in India and the Diaspora* (2011). The latter however happens much more later.

In 'Geo-politics, Dissensus, and Dance Citizenship: The Case of South Asian Dance in Britain' (2013), Avanthi Meduri discusses the 'label politics' and in particular the problematic and ambiguous history of the term 'South Asian Dance' with its 'dual focus on homogeneity and diversity.'[70] She reminds us that South Asia was created as a post-war geopolitical label in US foreign policy discourses, and describes how different British choreographers of 'South Asian' descent, 'wriggle creatively' within the label in order to secure themselves a (funded) position in the British dance landscape. Akram Khan's work wants to partially escape this politics of labeling. Andrée Grau quotes Farooq Chaudhry, the manager of the Akram Khan Company, as rejecting 'blanket terms like South Asian dance.'[71]

At the same time we should not forget that these 'new hybrid' forms have existed at all times. In 'Our Hybrid Tradition' (2000), Sally Banes's contribution to the conference 'Dance: Distinct Language and Cross-cultural Influences' (which was organized by the FIND in Montreal in 1999), she proves that the late twentieth-century fashion for intercultural exchange and cultural hybridization in world music and dance has a very long tradition.[72] Banes offers a very long, well-documented overview of choreographers being influenced in their work by 'the Other.' Going back to the beginnings of twentieth century Western modern dance, she shows how its pioneers Loie Fuller, Isadora Duncan, and Ruth Saint Denis all integrated elements of African and Asian dance which they discovered at the World's Fair in Paris in 1900. Other icons of twentieth-century Western dance, too, overtly borrowed or took their inspiration from other cultures: Mary Wigman using elements of different Japanese traditions in her *Witch Dance*, Martha Graham eclectically quoting from Asian, African-American, and Native American sources, George Balanchine renewing the ballet tradition by using elements deriving from African-American jazz dancing, Merce Cunningham's pure dance philosophy being based on Zen Buddhism and Confucianism, and Steve Paxton's contact improvisation being rooted in Aikido. She also gives plenty of examples of Western dance in its turn influencing Asian and African dance: Bollywood films incorporating 'jazz moves and hiphop inflected bhangra,' the Chinese ballet tradition being founded on its Russian predecessors and teachers, and Japanese Butoh being 'a thickly layered version of multiple hybridization.' She concludes: 'Dance fusions in both East and West have taken place in the context of hegemonic domination, of resistance to colonial and other forms of repression, of cultural collaboration, and of avant-garde exploration.'[73]

This last element of Banes's conclusion, the multiple reasons why artists borrow from other cultures and traditions, resonates with my own contribution to the conference: 'Dance: A Translating Art. The Body as a "Transmuter" of Identity' (2001). Defining the act of translation as the basis of any creative process where artists translate sources that inspire them into their own target language/medium, I describe how in the middle of the twentieth century, translation theory underwent a fundamental shift in perspective. Until then, translation theory had been mainly occupied with the notion and question of how one could be faithful to the original (often in the context of the translation of 'holy' religious texts) and the resulting problems of (un)translatability. But under the influence of thinkers such as Walter Benjamin with 'The Task of the Translator' (1923) and Jacques Derrida with, amongst others, 'Living On' (1979), priorities were reversed. The task of the translator/translation lies with one's own target language or culture, in that the introduction of new and foreign elements will have an innovative effect on one's own language, with the potential to change and evolve it. It has been my strong conviction that the creative process in contemporary art, and in dance in particular, is very much based on these insights of translation theory. Taking 'foreign' elements from another culture, another discipline, or another body and introducing them into one's own, creates a state of temporary 'confusion' out of which new insights and forms are generated.

In a lecture at the same FIND conference, entitled 'Moving Contexts' the American performer and dance scholar Ann Cooper Albright describes her own experiences with cross-cultural exchanges and border crossings from the different perspectives of performer, spectator, and scholar. In order to better understand the nature of border crossings, she defines two very different approaches. The first focuses on the analysis of how dancing is staged and how the meaning of this staging shifts across cultures. The second tries to describe the experience of 'the physical and metaphysical reverberation of another dance form within one's body as well as one's psyche.' She writes:

> This slippage between the lived body and its cultural repre-
> sentation, between what I call a somatic identity (the expe-
> rience of one's physicality) and a cultural one (how one's
> body—skin, gender, ability, age, etc.—renders meaning in

society) is the basis for what I consider some of the most interesting explorations of cultural identity in dance.[74]

Both Banes and Albright acknowledge the complexity of 'this slippage of cultural contexts' and the questions it raises about Orientalism, cultural appropriation, and authenticity. Albright for instance describes her experiences as a spectator of the notorious 1990 and 1993 Los Angeles Festivals curated by Peter Sellars, and asks herself if the festival, by giving visibility to non-Western dance forms, wasn't 'preserving a static notion of cultural identity, safely remaining within the colonial power dynamics of American culture.'[75] Meanwhile Banes concludes her contribution with the reflection that 'hybridity may itself be a way of hanging on to identity in a post-identity world—a way of claiming that there are still separate traditions available to be mixed.'[76]

Discussing the work of Congolese-Canadian choreographer Zab Maboungou, Albright suggests that 'her work re-fuses and con-fuses the polarization of contemporary and traditional labels' and that as a result of 'this borderland status' the work 'resists categorization' and is 'difficult to market.'[77] In 'Cultural Crossings: Containing the Crisis... and the Indian in our Midst' (2001), Stephanie Jordan discusses in a similar way the work of the British-Asian choreographer Shobana Jeyasingh, who has 'to negotiate a minefield of strategic alliances and shifting identities.'[78] Jordan quotes Jeyasingh describing her own artistic identity as a 'mix of David Bowie, Purcell, Shelley and Anna Pavlova, which has been mixed as subtly as samosa has mixed itself into the English cuisine [...] : impossible to separate.'[79]

This notion of confusion is also acknowledged by dancers and choreographers themselves, not only on the level of labelling their work but also on the level of their somatic experience and identity. Akram Khan and the South-African dancer George Mxolisi Khumalo, both of whom grew up and were educated in-between cultures and dance languages, describe their somatic experience as one of confusion. In an interview with Marianne Van Kerkhoven, titled 'Processes that Need Time' (2003), Khumalo describes how his body, being trained in South-African street dance, became confused after receiving contemporary, Western-oriented dance training at the Performing Arts Research and Training Studies (PARTS) in Brussels:

> The physical information I received at PARTS strongly influenced me, even more than I wanted. When I left PARTS in 2000, I felt very frustrated. The vocabulary my body used to carry had been replaced by the formal structures I had learnt in Brussels. [...] I felt I couldn't move anymore. I was afraid to do things. My body was confused and blocked. I started watching videos of things I had done in the past and I got the feeling I had lost everything. I tried to do as little as possible, as if I wanted to 'detox' all that information out of my body. I let my body go and information from the past gradually began to return. But it had been redefined; it fused together and was transformed by what I had learnt at PARTS. You need time for this sort of process, and to listen to your body.[80]

This confusion is not a new, amorphous entity from which the original sources have been erased. It is a fundamentally bipolar state that requires great technical ability and intuitive understanding in order to switch from one energy, one body, and one culture to another, allowing oneself to get temporarily lost in the process.

The creative potential of getting lost is also the 'crux' of the 'For a Sensorial Manifesto (On Dances that Failed)' (2001), André Lepecki's contribution to *Dance: Distinct Languages and Cross-Cultural Influences*. Lepecki gives the example of Barbara Brown, an American dance ethnographer and a 'blue-eyed American gringa' who, as she joins local dancers in Bahia, Brazil, is appreciated by them with an acknowledgment that 'she dances like a black.' Referencing Michael Taussig's *Mimesis and Alterity: A Particular History of the Senses* (1993), the example of Brown opens up for Lepecki the possibility of a sensorial manifesto that

> [...] rather than cutting up slices of social bodies into micro-identities of absolute differentiation [...] proposes a 'self losing itself, sinking, decomposing into the surrounding world, a yielding that is [...] an act of both imitation and of contact'. This is tremendously important—to act, to perform, to lose oneself into the world, to dis-identify, to decompose the boundaries of the difference-machine.[81]

At an early stage of his career as a 'contemporary' choreographer, Akram Khan rejects the notion that his work is about 'fusion.'

Fusion suggests blending together, eliminating and erasing the differences. Confusion, by contrast, is fusion to a higher degree, where you recognize and accept the differences, letting them co-exist and influence each other:

> In saying that his body became confused, Khan was recognizing that the effects of early training never disappear. Rather than trying to consciously combine these technical approaches, he chose instead to focus deeply, on the internal, somatic sources of dance movement within his neuro-skeleto-muscular continuum. To try to identify these sources as clearly as possible became a way of letting himself gradually discover how he could move.[82]

This somatic confusion is not very different from the one that always takes place whenever we let ourselves be contaminated or imprinted by the knowledge or qualities of another body. Except that in the case of the artist, the individual somatic experience becomes imbedded in a larger cultural and social context, attaining symbolic and exemplary value as a role model for cultural exchange even if it means having to negotiate confusion at intercultural and interpersonal levels. This negotiation is not always easy and might even result in conflict. In her essay 'Seeking the Self' (2008) Karthika Nair mentions at least one striking example of the latter in the work of Sidi Larbi Cherkaoui. In *Tempus Fugit*, dancers Lisi Estaràs (of Jewish-Argentinian descent) and Ali Thabet (with Tunisian roots) try to dance a ballroom dance together: 'one arches to tango while the other's shoulders involuntarily follow Oriental rhythms: they try communicating in separate tongues but the nascent attraction soon degenerates into what appears to be an Israeli-Palestinian slanging match.'[83] Uytterhoeven also describes this scene in detail and concludes: 'The duet between Estaràs and Thabet can be seen to represent many different kinds of inabilities to understand each other: those between men and women, between Palestinians and Israelis, between Muslim and non-Muslims, but ultimately also those between artist and audience. No resolution is offered.'[84]

This state of being 'lost in translation,' or the somatic confusion of two bodies interchanging, doesn't always have to be negative. It also has a huge creative potential waiting to be tapped into. Lorna Sanders, in her essay on *zero degrees* (2005), valorizes the notion of confusion, linking it explicitly to Bhabha's concept of a 'Third Space.' 'Bhabha's acknowledgement of ambivalence as inevitable to the analytical process provides another perspective on how I might see confusion as a positive construct which enables difference to emerge as productive and not problematic.'[85]

In the next chapter, I will try to illustrate the positive aspects of a somatic confusion in-between dance cultures by discussing in more detail a number of key productions in Sidi Larbi Cherkaoui's and Akram Khan's oeuvre. Although I am aware that the continuously expanding choreographic universes of both Larbi and Akram deal with many other themes, I will mainly focus on a number of creations that illustrate how they use their identity in-between cultures to create and stimulate a much-needed new social imagery. I will do so by combining my inside knowledge of their creative process (having accompanied them as a dance dramaturge on several of these creations) with aspects of performance and reception analysis. But before I dive into the work, I will give my own summary and rendering of their artistic biographies.

Notes

1 Burt 2007, p. 208.
2 *Berliner Zeitung*, 21 March, 2015.
3 Taken from the original European Union funding application of the project.
4 Franco 2007, pp. 3-4.
5 Grau 2007, pp. 199-201.
6 Grossberg 1996, p. 89.
7 Which forms the introduction to the book *Questions of Cultural Identity* (1996), edited by Stuart Hall and Paul du Gay.
8 Hall 1996, p. 1.
9 Ibid., pp. 2-4.
10 Bauman 1996, p. 18.
11 Strathern 1996, p. 40.
12 Robins 1996, p. 62.
13 Ibid., pp. 80-81.
14 Grossberg 1996, p. 89.
15 Ibid., pp. 90-93.
16 Bhabha 1996, p. 57.
17 Ibid., p. 58.
18 Bhabha 1994, p. 56.
19 Ibid., p. x.
20 Bhabha 2012, pp. 61-62.
21 Bhabha 1994, p. 31.
22 Hallam and Ingold 2007, p. 2.
23 Cherkaoui in Boisseau 2013, p.22.
24 De Somviele 2015. Only a couple of weeks later, Arts Centre Vooruit in Ghent, which is one of the leading arts centres for contemporary performance arts in Belgium, announced that they had engaged Khadija El Bennaoui, from Morocco, as their new artistic director. The two appointments happen at a time when the NVA, the ruling party in both the Flemish and federal government, is pushing a conservative, nationalistic agenda.
25 www.mo.be.
26 Cherkaoui 2014, January.
27 This story of his name was told during a lecture Faustin Linyekula gave at the Institute of Interweaving Performance Cultures of the Freie Universität, Berlin, 12 March 2015.
28 Bhabha 1994, p. 312.
29 Cherkaoui 2014, March.
30 Sibony 1991, p. 15.
31 Ibid., pp. 340-341.
32 Ibid., p. 13.
33 Ibid., p. 341.
34 Ibid., p. 31.
35 Ibid., p. 41.
36 Ibid., p. 232.
37 Ibid., p. 305.
38 Ingold 2011, pp. 150-154.
39 Akram Khan in Cools, 2012b, pp. 5-6.
40 Foster 2011, pp. 75-76.
41 Cherkaoui 2006b, pp. 45-46.
42 Cherkaoui in Boisseau 2013, p. 20.
43 Cherkaoui in Cools 2006, p. 38.
44 Levy 2014, p. 77.
45 Sibony 1995, pp. 89-90.
46 Delmas 2012.
47 Kristeva 2014, p. 86.
48 Instead of 'aspects,' Malouf uses the term 'appartenances,' 'belonging' to a larger group with whom we share that aspect of our identity.
49 Grau 2007, p. 191.
50 Malouf 1998, p. 34.
51 Ibid., p. 121.
52 Ibid., p. 160.
53 Cherkaoui 2008, p. 4.
54 Ibid., p. 8. For a critical discussion of the origin and the use of the label 'Flemish Dance Wave' see also Gielen and Laermans, 2000.
55 Cherkaoui 2008, p. 9.
56 Bogart 2014, p. 9.
57 Assmann 2000, p. 76.
58 Chambers 1994, p. 25.
59 Ingold 2011, pp. 160-161.
60 Bogart 2014, p. 97.
61 Keleman 1999, p. 6.
62 Ibid., p. 7.
63 Sennett 2011, p. 75.
64 Keleman 1999, p. 68.
65 Cherkaoui in Cools 2012a, pp. 19-21.
66 Uytterhoeven 2013, pp. 119-120.
67 Khan in Cools 2012b, pp. 25-26.
68 Ibid., pp. 15-16.
69 Burt 2004. See also Mitra 2010 for an excellent rendering of this 'diasporic account.'
70 Meduri 2013, p. 178.
71 Grau 2004.
72 In her introduction to the book *The Politics of Interweaving Performance* (2014), Erika Fischer-Lichte gives a similar overview of 'intercultural' theatre practices.
73 Banes 2000, pp. 28-29.
74 Albright 2000, p. 47.
75 Ibid., pp. 45-46.
76 Banes 2000, p. 30.
77 Albright 2000, pp. 48-49.
78 Jordan 2001, p. 115.
79 Ibid., p. 113.
80 Khumalo 2003, p. 8.
81 Lepecki 2001, pp. 166-167.
82 Burt 2004, p. 9.
83 Nair 2008, p. 113.
84 Uytterhoeven 2013, p. 176.
85 Sanders 2005.

Two Intertwined Artistic Journeys

A professional biography is also a story. As our career advances, we not only add facts and events but also occasionally erase some. We highlight certain achievements and downplay others. We adapt our CV according to our future job aspirations and how we want others to perceive our professional identity. An artist's CV in particular, leading a more public life in programme brochures or catalogues, press announcements and interviews, is always a carefully cultivated construction. Eventually it might itself become canonized, part of art history, or it might be rewritten in future biographies or even biopics. The biographies of Sidi Larbi Cherkaoui and Akram Khan are no exception to this. What follows is my personal account of their careers. I draw on the approved official versions of their CVs and will from time to time add some 'apocryphal' facts.

Sidi Larbi Cherkaoui: A Chameleon Absorbing Other Dance Cultures and Languages

> I trust more and more the flexibility of my own body to take on different shapes and colors like a chameleon.[1]

In 2007, the new National Museum for the History of Immigration in Paris commissions a video installation from Sidi Larbi Cherkaoui and French visual artist and filmmaker Gilles Delmas.[2] They create the piece *Zon-Mai* (2007). Larbi describes how, on his first visit to the site, he is emotionally affected by the paradox between its history and its new mission:

> The foundational idea behind this new institution is opposite to its original mission. The original project was based on an ethnocentric vision where Europe imposed itself on the periphery and talked about everything that came from elsewhere from a Western point of view. The new project affirms that we are no longer at the center [...] and this implies a process of relearning to think and to work.[3]

Zon-Mai is the perfect physical and visual metaphor to summarize Larbi's artistic CV and the underlying vision of his work. On the four walls and the roof of an abstract house ('maison' in French) twenty-one short choreographic films are projected, presenting dancers from eighteen different countries, all migrants in their temporary 'homes.' Their number, twenty-one, mirrors the number of Major Arcana in a tarot deck:

> Dancers from very different backgrounds—geographically and artistically—with very distinct energies reunite under the same roof. [...] I didn't simply want to underline that all these worlds co-exist in the same space-time continuum. I also wanted to escape the usual ritual of beginnings and ends. Having put all the sequences in a loop, I wanted to show that life doesn't have a beginning or end. It continues. It is an irresistible succession of transformations.[4]

Larbi's short description of *Zon-Mai* could equally stand for his whole choreographic oeuvre.

Sidi Larbi Cherkaoui is born in 1976 as the second son of a Flemish mother and a Moroccan father. His parents meet in a local bar in Hoboken, the Antwerp suburb where he grows up and goes to high school, enjoying studying both mathematics and languages. At home they speak Dutch, French and Arabic, and he is taught the foundations of both the Catholic and the Muslim faith. When he is fifteen, his parents divorce and his father returns to Morocco, where he dies from a heart attack soon after.

From the very beginning of his dance career, Sidi Larbi Cherkaoui is an autodidact, always looking for the best teachers in an eclectic range of dance techniques which he absorbs and makes his own. In his early formative years, he studies amongst others jazz dance and ballet. He spends only one year at the Performing Arts Research and Training Studies (PARTS), the dance school founded by Anne Teresa De Keersmaeker, before moving on to find teachers all over the world. Larbi is a huge believer in the idea that you can learn anything at any age, as long as you completely dedicate yourself to it and invest enough time in it. 'As an artist and as a human being, I see my life as a never interrupted learning process.'[5] His favourite learning strategy is imitating the 'master,' and he continues to seek out masters from different music and dance traditions. Some of the art forms he has trained in and entered into conversation with include Kathak, Kuchipudi, flamenco, tango, Shaolin Kung Fu, Chinese pole climbing, puppeteering, kabuki theatre, Corsican polyphonic singing, and playing the piano and the harp.

He makes his debut as a dancer in variety shows and popular television programs. In 1995, he is discovered by the contemporary dance scene when he wins the competition for the Best Belgian Dance Solo organized by Alain Platel from Les Ballets C de la B, who subsequently invites him to perform in *Iets op Bach* [Something on Bach] (1997). While dancing with Les Ballets C de la B, Larbi also starts to develop his choreographic interest, by signing up to choreograph a contemporary musical. *Anonymous Society* (1999), by the Irish director Andrew Wale, is based on the songs of Jacques Brel. The two will team up again in 2005, when they create another musical, *Some Girls are Bigger than Others* (2005), this time based on the work of Morrissey and The Smiths.

Sidi Larbi Cherkaoui makes his official choreographic debut with *Rien de Rien* (2000), produced by Les Ballets C de la B, who will continue to offer him a creative home-base until 2006, when he becomes artist in residence of the Toneelhuis in Antwerp. From this debut onward, Sidi Larbi Cherkaoui will systematically promote the non-hierarchical coexistence of different dance languages and cultures that characterizes his work to this day. Formally it translates into an eclectic style where medieval polyphonic music coexists with pop songs, and where any kind of dance technique is given equal value as long as it contributes to the 'story being told.' 'The essence of my work,' he states, 'is the communication and the dialogue with the audience. Sometimes you don't have words to express yourself and then you dance. Sometimes it can't be danced and then you sing. Sometimes it can't be sung and then you tell it.'[6]

Rien de Rien already contains all the stylistic characteristics and themes that he will continue to explore and develop in his quickly expanding oeuvre and universe. The set of *Rien de Rien* is a stylized version of a mosque. Written on the back wall in Arabic calligraphy is: 'Prohibitions stir desire.' Possibly this is a subliminal message to his dead father, who disapproved of both his homosexuality and his desire to pursue a dance career. The voice of the muezzin is replaced by a cellist, Roel Dieltiens, who performs amongst others work by György Ligeti. The classical music enters into a dialogue with early Italian polyphonic music, as well as with a jazzy pop song. Six dancers between the age of fourteen and sixty—including his lifelong artistic partner Damien Jalet and his former ballet teacher Marie-Louise Wilderijckx—perform an eclectic range of dance techniques ranging from hip hop to ball-room dancing and ballet, including his signature choreography of the natural hand movements that accompany our talking. The theme of intercultural exchange is already very present, in a relativizing and humouristic way. Angélique Wilkie, a Jamaican-Canadian performer, tells the story of her voyage to Africa and the cultural misunderstandings resulting from this change of perspective. *Rien de Rien* embarks on a two-year-long world tour and immediately establishes Sidi Larbi Cherkaoui as one of the choreographic talents of the new millennium. Les Ballets C de la B supports the production of a succession of new creations: *Corpus Bach* (2006), *zero degrees* (2005), *Tempus Fugit* (2004), and *Foi* (2003), allowing Sidi Larbi to create his own 'family' of likeminded artists, a lot of whom he continues to collaborate with to this day.

Foi is another piece that gains iconic status. Situated in the historical moment between the aftermath of 9/11 and the eve of Iraq War, it marks the first decade of the twenty-first century. A no man's land, reminiscent of Ground Zero, is populated by the dead and missing victims of a disaster and their guardian angels. Flashes of concrete images—a mother searching for her lost child, a bird caught in a patch of oil, a pair of boxing gloves with the American flag on them, a dancer in lotus position who could either be a meditating Buddha or a crippled martyr, or both—are juxtaposed to create a multilayered, poetic dance universe.

Parallel to his work with Les Ballets C de la B, Sidi Larbi Cherkaoui also begins to engage with major ballet companies as a guest choreographer. He creates *In Memoriam* (2004) and *Mea Culpa* (2006) for Les Ballets de Monte Carlo, and *Loin* (2005) for the Ballet du Grand Théâtre de Genève. In *Mea Culpa* (2006), he highlights the stereotypical gender archetypes of ballet, as well as opens up neglected questions of race. The black dancers in the company are cast as servants who clean the floor or become a pedestal for the others to sit on. While the 'white' cast, dressed in Karl Lagerfeld and toasting each other with champagne, parties in the centre of the stage, the periphery of the space overflows with garbage. A screen at the back shows projected images of Senegal. Cherkaoui directly addresses the colonial guilt and responsibility of his hosts, the Grimaldis, and holds a dire mirror up to his glamorous premiere audience.

Other such 'side projects' turn out to be not only extremely successful but also very formative. *D'Avant* (2002), created with Damien Jalet, Juan Kruz Diaz de Garaio Esnaola, and Luc Dunberry,[7] allows Sidi Larbi Cherkaoui to deepen his understanding and mastery of polyphonic singing as a complementary way of dancing. Larbi discovers the unique qualities of polyphonic singing as a way to tune into different voices and bodies through Jalet, who introduces him to the Belgian singer Christine Leboutte. Together, the three embark on a journey through different polyphonic traditions. They will be joined amongst others by Jean-Claude Acquaviva of the Corsican group A Filetta and by Patrizia Bovi and her Ensemble Micrologus (from Italy), who will not only accompany several productions but also co-create the musical dramaturgy for them. More than ten years after its creation, *D'Avant* is still being performed on dance stages around the world.

With Nienke Reehorst, who will be his choreographic assistant for many years, he co-creates *Ook* (2002) for Theater Stap, a professional theatre company with performers who have Down's syndrome. Through it he discovers the exceptional talent of these performers, who combine empathy, straightforwardness, and dedication, and he decides to invite some of them to participate in his own work.

From 2006 to 2010, Sidi Larbi Cherkaoui is artist in residence at Toneelhuis in Antwerp, invited by artistic director Guy Cassiers, for whom he will also choreograph the dance sections of Wagner's *Ring* cycle at the Scala in Milan and the Staatsoper in Berlin. During this period he creates *Myth* (2007) and *Origine* (2008). At the same time he develops a privileged relationship with both La Monnaie (the national opera house in Brussels) and Sadler's Wells Theatre in London. They will respectively produce *Apocrifu* (2007) and his first opera *Shell Shock* (2014), as well as *Sutra* (2008), *TeZukA* (2011), and *Milonga* (2013).

For his quartet *Origine*, Sidi Larbi Cherkaoui consciously chooses four dancers whose countries of origin literally represent the four cardinal directions: Valgerður Vala Rúnarsdóttir from Iceland, Shawn Mothupi from South Africa, Daisy Phillips from the US, and Kazutomi 'Tsuki' Kozuki from Japan. The final image of this ode to the interconnectedness of life on this planet is the globe of Google Earth erasing the multiplicity of individual files and messages on a desktop screen. But before we arrive there, Shawn has been exposed to forced medical examinations and biometric tests and has to walk blindfolded on a projected map which becomes increasingly crumpled. Tsuki's body becomes completely 'objectified' in a virtuosic dance mime in which he transforms himself into all the commodities that Daisy needs.

Sidi Larbi Cherkaoui likes to compare his artistic identity to a chameleon or shape-shifter. His choreographic universe is full of such transformations, where the images that the body creates change continuously, and where we move fluidly from one dance language to another. 'I looked for how a floor movement could transform to a jump or how an African dance could mutate into an Irish one. How if you change two or three elements, things come together. Two or three changes are enough for me to become another, who at first sight looks so different.'[8]

In 2010, Sidi Larbi Cherkaoui finally founds his own company, Eastman, which is funded by the Flemish government and has a permanent home in deSingel International Arts Campus in Antwerp. With Eastman he creates amongst others: *Babel*[words] (2010), co-directed with Jalet; *Play* (2010), co-directed with Shantala Shivalingappa; *Puz/zle* (2012); and *Genesis* 生长 (2013) in collaboration with Yabin Wang and the Yabin Dance Studio in Beijing. In *Play*, Sidi Larbi Cherkaoui absorbs elements of Shivalingippa's Kuchipudi dance technique. Whenever he learns a new language, it is not with the intention or pretence of becoming a master of this technique. He mainly wants to give his body a new experience and allow it to transform. *Play* thematically deals with the polarities of female and male energies, without fixing or defining them. It consciously remains playful, engaging in games of seduction but also in a real chess game. As in many of Cherkaoui's productions, there is a strong focus on the articulatedness of the hands. Both the movement vocabulary and the music again celebrate an extreme eclecticism.

For a long period, the main focus in Sidi Larbi Cherkaoui's work has been the question of identity and the parallels between religion and performance as rituals for connecting people. He himself has called it his 'social period,' with productions that consciously aim at a political and critical content. In his more recent works, such as *Puz/zle* or *Genesis* 生长, he also focuses on the body itself and its relationship with other materials, for instance, stones in *Puz/zle* or crystals in *Genesis* 生长. 'They are all ways to research how the body will react when it touches certain materials. How these materials inspire us physically if we touch them.'[9] This evolution in Cherkaoui's work has been inspired amongst others by his collaborations with the visual artist Antony Gormley, with whom he worked on *zero degrees*, *Sutra*, *Babel*^(words), and *Noetic* (2014). Gormley investigates the energetic qualities of the body and the different materials with which he works. His sculptural and scenic proposals always inspire Cherkaoui to move them. In the four productions for which they have collaborated, there is a clear sense of evolution: in *zero degrees*, the 'dummies' still represent the human body as an object to be manipulated; in *Sutra*, the wooden boxes define the space around the body and are used as building blocks to continuously create new images (a temple, an island, a ship, a lotus flower); in *Babel*^(words) the frames represent the spatial boundaries we draw in society, which, as the work shows, can be moved; and in *Noetic*, the carbon fibre lines constantly bend under the movement of the dancers serving as a metaphor for our experience of nothing ever being entirely straightforward.

Puz/zle which is created for the Carrière de Boulbon, the quarry in Avignon where Peter Brook presented his version of the *Mahabharata* (1985), tells the history of humankind through its relationship with stones: from the biblical parable of 'he who throws the first stone' to the edifices we build, to the body fossilizing once again into its skeleton. In *Puz/zle* there is also a shift from the individual body to the collective body. As James Surowiecki describes in *The Wisdom of the Crowds* (2004), the group is always more intelligent than the individual and it is through collective collaboration that we are able to literally rise above ourselves. In *Puz/zle* we are also inside the body, looking at the movements at the level of DNA and cells: how for instance the telomere separate at both ends of the DNA and thus cause a loss of information—the essence of our aging process. We travel through the history of human civilization, a continuous process of growth and decay, of destruction and rebuilding of monuments we erect as silent witnesses of the past. And we listen to the cosmic dance of the stones that are the planets: the music of the spheres. The latter is probably also the origin of the stone labyrinths that we find in all cultures and which are thought to be a choreographic pattern for a spiral dance, celebrating the connection between man and the universe. *Puz/zle* doesn't hide the violence of this ongoing cycle of death and rebirth, but it celebrates how transformation always happens through an act of imagination and the willpower accompanying it. How human curiosity might accidentally trigger change.

From his very first creation *Rien de Rien* onward, the wall is a recurrent theme in Sidi Larbi Cherkaoui's work—the wall as a symbol for the boundaries we install between ourselves and the other, in Berlin, in Israel, on the borders of 'Fort Europa.' But we also build walls around our own gardens. And our skin has evolved from a porous contact zone to a hygienic wall of its own. As a result we often literally 'hit the wall' of our own egos and our own limits, both as individuals and as a society. For real transformation to happen we have to bring down these walls, even if this process involves the possibility of (self-)destruction.

Today, Eastman is the centre of Cherkaoui's ever-expanding artistic universe, which includes further ballet commissions such as *End* (2006) for the Cullberg Ballet, *L'Homme de bois* (2007) for the Royal Danish Ballet, or *Labyrinth* (2011) for the Dutch National Ballet. He also collaborates with the British director Joe Wright on theatre and film projects, amongst others the feature film *Anna Karenina* (2012). Other projects include choreography for the Cirque du Soleil and a music video for the Icelandic band Sigur Rós. All of this culminates in his appointment as artistic director of the Royal Flemish Ballet, a position he will combine with directing his own company from autumn 2015 onward.

The diversity of his artistic universe is a perfect illustration of his non-hierarchical, inclusive philosophy that rejects simple classifications and traditional boundaries such as those between 'high' and 'popular' art. If you look more closely at his entire oeuvre, you also start to notice how its different strands complement each other: the work with Eastman and his own core group of collaborators feeds into his exchange projects with other artists in which he learns a new (dance) language, which in turn inspire and enrich the commissioned work. In what follows I will focus on three creations: *zero degrees*, *Myth*, and *Babel*(words), which all deal with the polarities of an identity in-between cultures.

Akram Khan: Being Rooted in One Dance Culture

> You have to be rooted in your own culture in order to be able to sense and understand another one deeply enough to make it your own.[10]

In 2008 the National Portrait Gallery in London commissions the American-Iranian painter Darvish Fakhr to paint a portrait of Akram Khan. In dialogue with Akram, Fakhr chooses to paint the portrait applying the Indian principle of *rasa*, that is, to depict Akram not in a single pose but nine times, each time embodying a different emotion or mood associated with the aesthetic experience of rasa: *sringara* [love], *vira* [heroism], *rudra* [anger], *bibhatsa* [disgust], *hasya* [humour], *adbhuta* [wonder], *karuna* [pathos], *bhayanaka* [terror], and *shanta* [serenity]. In order to capture them, Fakhr films Akram during the rehearsals of *bahok* (2008) and uses stills from the video for the different postures. The nine miniature portraits are all painted in sepia brown, earthy colours, with Akram alternately wearing a black or white T-shirt. The different moods are conveyed not so much through his facial expressions—he often looks down, has his eyes closed, or even shows only the back of his head—but instead are captured in the virtuosic, dynamic, and choreographed gestures of his hands and arms: for instance giving the viewer the finger at the back of his head in anger, or pulling his head upward with a serene hand mudra. Yet Fakhr's aim is not to paint a simple one-to-one correspondence between portrait and emotion. 'I thought emotions could be like cocktails instead—courage mixed with fear. One person might see wonder in one of the panels, another might see anger. It's not so black and white.'[11] Fakhr is consciously looking for a sense of 'in-betweenness,' which is best illustrated by the middle portrait, the only one in which Akram stares directly at the viewer, with his arms strangely contortioned around his head and one hand, in a reversed mudra, covering one eye.

Akram Khan is born in 1974 into a Bangladeshi family of migrants, who have moved to the United Kingdom after Bangladesh's independence in 1971 and now live in Wimbledon in South London. His mother is a schoolteacher, and his father an accountant and restaurant owner. In all his public interviews, Akram has always acknowledged the importance of his mother in both introducing him to Kathak, which is the only Indian dance form that has both Hindu and Muslim influences, and in guiding his career as a dancer and choreographer. One can only guess why she sends him to his first folk dance classes at a young age, and from the age of seven to learn Kathak under the guidance of Sri Pratap Pawar, one of the most celebrated Kathak masters in the world.[12] Is it because she has unfulfilled dance ambitions herself, as Akram suggests in the interview I quoted in the previous chapter? Is it because she senses the exceptional potential in her hyperactive child? Or is her choice motivated by a more clichéd kind of diasporic nostalgia:Is she trying to create a link to her homeland and culture?

In the past decade many, mainly Indian, dance scholars, have critically discussed both the 'cleansing' of Indian dance styles as part of a nationalistic agenda and the adoption of the term 'classical' as being 'motivated by the desire to give recognizable national and international status to the dance that was being reconstituted.'[13] In her contribution to *Worlding Dance* (2009), Ananya Chatterjea also critically analyzes 'how "classical dances" were repeatedly legitimized through appropriation by the urban elite'[14] and how 'the North-South classical bind of the bharatnatyam (from the South) or kathak (from the North) model swallowed up the multiplicity and regional heterogeneity' of other dance forms.[15] They are right in their analysis, but it doesn't change the fact that for Akram's mother and her generational peers in the Indian diaspora, as well as for his audiences both in Britain and India, these categorizations and generalizations have been relevant 'realities.'

Akram Khan quickly turns into the child prodigy his mother suspected him to be. Already at the age of ten he is performing in *The Adventures of Mowgli* (based on Rudyard Kipling's story collection *The Jungle Book* (1894) and best known as the 1967 Walt Disney adaptation), which also features Pandit Ravi Shankar, who tells Akram's father to ensure his son gets every opportunity to dance. The production is commissioned by the Academy of Indian Dance, established in the late seventies to promote South-Asian dance in the UK. Four years later, he spends two years touring the world in Peter Brook's epic but controversial version of the *Mahabharata* (1985), all the time continuing to practice his Kathak technique with his 'guruji.' In *Sacred Monsters* (2007), the duet he creates with Sylvie Guillem, he will look back on these formative years: the strict rigor of working under the guidance of a master and the burden of the public expectations that 'stardom' at a young age implies. But these experiences also prepare him well for his future professional career in which he continues to combine a dedicated work ethic with both a celebration of and a perspective on his status as a 'sacred monster.'

At the age of eighteen, he is formally presented by Sri Pratap Pawar in his first solo recital, marking the completion of a first cycle of formation. In *An Artist of the Floating World* (1986),

Kazuo Ishiguro describes in detail the complicated relationship between a master and his disciple within an Asian context. If the pupil leaves the master too soon, he won't be equipped to become a master himself. If he leaves too late, he will remain an epigone all his life. A skilled master and a talented disciple know when the moment of separation has arrived and are able to enact the necessary rupture.

Shortly after this recital, Akram Khan embarks on a new formative cycle, studying first at De Montfort University, Leicester from 1994–1996 and eventually graduating from the Northern School of Contemporary Dance, Leeds in 1998. He adds to his knowledge of Kathak a training in ballet and the main techniques of modern and contemporary dance, including Graham, Cunningham, release technique and contact improvisation. It is in this second cycle that he begins to discover the challenges but also the creative potential of the somatic confusion arising from moving in-between dance languages.

While still studying, he makes his first contemporary dance solos *Loose in Flight* (1995) and *Fix* (1995), which are still firmly rooted in the Kathak vocabulary and often presented in a mixed bill with more traditional Kathak material. *Loose in Flight* is filmed for the Channel Four dance film series *Per4mance*. The Kathak vocabulary is stripped of its narrative and religious connotations and combined with typical nineties 'eurotrash' moves such as dives and rolls on the floor. The whole film is literally displaced, set within the industrial landscape of the London Docklands, a feature common to a lot of the dance films of the 1990s. Another formative influence is British choreographer Jonathan Burrows, who Akram meets when participating in the influential UK International Choreographic Course for Choreographers and Composers. Burrows mentors the creation of *Fix* and also invites Akram to create a duet together, *Duet* (1999), which is only performed once, at *Desert Steps*, an evening celebrating the fiftieth anniversary of composer Kevin Volans at the Southbank Centre.[16] In 2000, Akram Khan is invited to participate in the X-group, a residency program for young choreographers at the Performing Arts Research and Training Studies (PARTS), part of Brussels's programme during its year as the European Capital of Culture. Akram uses the residency to create his first group piece, the trio *Rush* (2000), in which, for the first time, he transfers his movement vocabulary and skills to other bodies.[17]

This notion of transfer of somatic knowledge will remain important throughout his career as a way to teach but also to learn.

Already at this early point in his career, his teacher Pawar advises Akram to also develop a teaching practice, since 'teaching is an important part of learning' and 'allows you to re-examine your own beliefs.'[18] Akram takes this advice to heart and starts teaching Sunday Kathak lessons to six- and seven-year-olds. From the early days of his company onward, he will also offer his dancers and musicians further training. The charity AKCT (an acronym for Advanced Kathak and Choreographic Training) is created alongside his dance company for this exact purpose. In the autumn of 2005, AKCT organizes the first edition of *The Bi-Lingual Dancer* workshop programme, in order to pass on Akram's knowledge of Kathak as a source for a contemporary arts practice to other dancers and musicians. As teachers, Akram invites, next to himself, the Indian Kathak master Kumudini Lakhia and the composers Thierry De Mey and Matteo Fargion. The group of fourteen participants includes no less than nine different nationalities: British, Indian, Chinese, Korean, Malaysian, Thai, Spanish, Slovakian, and South African, which raises the question of whether the use of 'bi-lingual' in the title is well chosen. After all these dancers and musicians are artistic polyglots who master a variety of techniques and who are now invited to explore and add to their already versatile repertoire at least one other: Kathak.

Every morning the workshop starts with a Kathak class, given by Lakhia. She introduces the different parts of the technique's vocabulary in an analytical way: the footwork (*tatkar*), the codified hand gestures (*hastas* or *mudras*), the spins (*chakkar*), all of which she quickly integrates into more complex choreographic structures. Parallel to teaching the 'moves' of Kathak, she also initiates the participants into the underlying ideas and philosophy of the Indian dance, for instance the aesthetic principle of tihai ('thirdness' or 'three times'): following a certain beat, you repeat every composition three times—the first time 'to hear' it, the second time 'to recognize' it, the third time 'to give yourself over to it' and 'to be moved by' it. As one of the great twentieth-century innovators of the 'rather loose' Kathak tradition,[19] Kumudini Lakhia was one of the first to approach her tradition in a scientific and analytical way: respecting the geography of the body, introducing mathematical principles, and simplifying its ornaments (for instance the costume) to their essence. But when passing it on to a younger generation of performers, she is able to teach them both the rigour of her own practice and to allow them the freedom to incorporate and re-actualize the Kathak vocabulary within their own contemporary approaches.

A second class every morning introduces different contemporary approaches and techniques and is aimed at creating an exchange between the different forms of body knowledge that the participants already have. In the afternoon, Fargion and De Mey, accompanied by Akram Khan and myself, guide the participants in choreographic composition exercises whose purpose is at least a two-fold: to further integrate the Kathak vocabulary into a contemporary approach, and to stimulate the dancers and musicians to be more articulate themselves, to give them 'a voice.' In order to achieve an interweaving of dance languages, the participants are asked to make up a movement phrase to a popular folk song, integrating the Kathak vocabulary that they have learnt in the morning class. They then teach this phrase to the other dancers and afterward transform it by applying various different compositional principles and techniques. Over a period of only two weeks, the workshop proves how the combination of 'being rooted in one language' and the openness of a contemporary, creative mind to transform and actualize this language, can lead to amazing results, both on the individual level of the performer and within a larger, creative group process.

By this stage of his career, Akram Khan has already assembled around him a group of collaborators that he will continue to work with to this day, among them the composer Nitin Sawhney and the lighting designer Michael Hulls. Pivotal in the further development of his company is the close collaboration and association with dance producer Farooq Chaudhry. Chaudhry is of Pakistani origin and is himself an ex-dancer, having worked with amongst others Joachim Schlömer and Anne Teresa De Keersmaeker before retraining in arts management. They meet in 1999, as Akram is taking his very first steps in his development as a choreographer. Chaudhry takes on the risk of founding and managing the Akram Khan Company, mortgaging his own house to do so. From then on, the two will develop Akram Khan's career and work together, strategically and in constant close dialogue about how to combine artistic choices with, for the dance world, innovative business models.

One of their strategies is to associate themselves with other successful artists in the UK that belong to the Indian/Asian diaspora, collaborating for example with Sawhney on *Fix* (1995), *Kaash* (2002), *zero degrees* (2005), and *bahok* (2008), with the visual artist Anish Kapoor on *Kaash* (2002), and *in-i* (2008), with the writer Hanif Kureishi on *Ma* (2004), and with the poet Kathika Nair on *Desh* (2011) and *Until the Lions* (2016). It is a conscious, ongoing strategy to employ collaborators with an international background at all levels of the company, from dancers to management. 'The make-up of our workforce is international. A lot of artists come from different cultures and that is almost kind of in our DNA—we do select very interesting people from different places to bring their language, their point of view and perspective to ours to find a third way.'[20]

Kaash (2002) is Akram Khan's first full-length piece.[21] Its creation is finalized during a residence at the Arts Centre Vooruit in Ghent. One of its main sources is Amaury de Riencourt's *Eye of Shiva: Eastern Mysticism and Science* (1980), which is given to Akram by Kapoor. In this comparative study of Western and Eastern philosophy, science and religion, De Riencourt describes how, after man left behind his magical, embodied relationship with the world as expressed in mythical language in order to develop a scientific consciousness, East and West developed in opposite directions. The West focused on the external world and attempted to objectify reality, while the East turned inward, trying to understand the Self as part of a fundamentally subjective reality. Abstract and rhythmical, *Kaash* explores the parallels between Indian mythology, such as Shiva's cycle of creation and destruction, and Western physics, such as Stephen Hawking's theory of black holes.

From *Ma* in 2004 onward, Akram Khan begins to integrate more narrative and theatrical elements into his dance universe. *Ma,* which stands both for 'mother' and 'earth/nature,' is an ecological dance parable set to a story by Kureishi of a woman who can't bear children and nurtures trees instead. In it, Akram also (re)introduces the live music that accompanies his Kathak recitals. Kathak is in essence a structured improvisation between the soloist dancer and the musicians accompanying him. While the feet are engaged in a rhythmic dialogue with the tabla player, the hands enact the stories narrated by the singer.

Parallel to his early group creations, which remain firmly rooted in Kathak technique, Akram continues to dance solo

Kathak recitals such as *Polaroid Feet* (2001), *ronin* (2003), *third catalogue* (2005), and *Gnosis* (2009). The latter three all include a staged version of *Mahabahrata* tales. From the very beginning, Akram's Kathak recitals are described by the critics as 'contemporary kathak,'[22] and it is one of the merits of his career that the 'contemporary' work and the 'kathak' work are no longer considered as separate categories but that both are equally presented next to each other on the major international dance stages.

With *zero degrees*, his exchange with Sidi Larbi Cherkaoui, Akram initiates a third strand in his expanding choreographic universe. This third strand will be a series of 'dialogues' in which he enters into somatic exchanges with other major artists and performers. *zero degrees* is followed by *Sacred Monsters* with Sylvie Guillem and *in-i* (2008) with Juliette Binoche. 'Even though the common denominator of these three works is my body in duet with another body, my body is changing because of them. Whether I want to change or not is irrelevant because being in contact with someone who is so different brings out another side of you.'[23] The more recent duet *Torobaka* (2014), with flamenco dancer Israel Galván, inscribes itself into the same strand, as does the duet with the Japanese taiko drummer and dancer Yoshie Sunahata, which is part of *Gnosis* (2009). In both these duets two dance and performance cultures are intricately interwoven: Kathak with flamenco in the former, and tales from the *Mahabharata* with kabuki themes in the latter.

bahok, a co-production between the Akram Khan Company and the National Ballet of China that is part of the cultural program leading up to the 2008 Summer Olympics in Beijing, is probably the production that deals most with the issue of identity and intercultural dialogue. It is also my last collaboration with Akram Khan as a dramaturge. From then on he will collaborate with the UK-based Australian dramaturge Ruth Little. The group pieces that follow also shift—both in content and form. The topic of identity moves to the background and is replaced by themes of spirituality in *vertical road* (2010) and Stravinsky's music and biography in *itmoi* (2013). Formally they become less narrative and theatrical, now being based mainly on long, intricate, and complex dance sections where the visual and physical metaphors (as expressed for example in costumes and props) replace text and stories. The latter he keeps for his solo *Desh*. After the series of duets and exchanges with other bodies, Akram feels a strong desire to reconnect with his own body and (hi)story. *Desh* is an in-depth exploration of his relationship with Bangladesh. In what follows I will discuss it in more detail, next to *bahok* and *zero degrees*.

From 2012, Akram Khan also starts to accept commissions from other companies and for events, including: choreographing part of the opening ceremony for the 2012 Summer Olympics in London, *Dust* (2014) for the English National Ballet, the choreography for the feature film *Desert Dancer* (2014), curating the visual arts exhibition *One Side to the Other* for the Lowry gallery in Manchester (2014–2015), and creating a new piece for Guillem's final programme and farewell to her extraordinary dance career with *Life in Progress* (2015).

In his latest production, *Until the Lions* (2016), which is due to premiere at the Roundhouse in London in January 2016, Akram Khan will continue to explore his own cultural heritage. *Until the Lions* is a partial adaptation of Nair's reworking of the *Mahabharata* with the focus more on the characters than on the 'tales.' In *Until the Lions*, Akram will explore in particular the tale of the princess Amba who, abducted on her wedding day, invokes the Gods to seek revenge:

> In these compelling stories, the figures that lingered in my memory the most have been the female characters—often the unsung heroes, figures of strength and imagination and endurance. *Until the Lions* is our attempt to revisit the story of such an unsung hero, Amba, and to explore the notion and physical expression of gender and the baggage that comes with it—issues that we are all too often discouraged from exploring and debating in South Asian society.[24]

zero degrees (2005): The Serendipity of a Meeting

> I met them first in a land where borders
> get blurred; where day rises before night's end
> and water morphs into high, brumal walls.
> A warrior and a monk, two beings —
> flanked by shadows that grow and roam at will —
> cross-legged in thought, carving with four hands[25]

At several points in the documentary *zero degrees, infinity* (2006), which Gilles Delmas makes during the piece's creation process,

Sidi Larbi Cherkaoui and Akram Khan define zero degrees as 'the place in-between,' 'the no-man's land in-between frontiers,' 'the transition in-between life and death,' and 'the place in-between when two people meet or separate.'

Sidi Larbi Cherkaoui and Akram Khan meet early on in their careers as contemporary choreographers. Akram approaches Larbi when he is looking for dancers for his first group piece, *Rush* (2000), but Larbi has already launched his own choreographic career, which takes off immediately following his first production *Rien de Rien* (2000). Already during this first contact they sense a huge potential for further exchange and discover similarities and differences in both their personal and artistic journeys. They decide to continue to meet regularly: firstly to see and to get to know each other's work, secondly to discuss their shared interests and convictions, and finally also to spend some time together in the studio to see whether they can find a common physical ground from which to create.

From an early stage in their encounter, Akram and Larbi are not only aware of their similarities but also of their differences. In the original program text of *zero degrees* (2005), I summarize this as follows:

> The two have much in common. They belong to the same generation. They both hover between their traditional ethnic (Indian and Moroccan) and religious (Muslim) roots and the contemporary Western society they grew up in. Neither of them drink alcohol and they both invest the resulting, surplus energy in their creative work (which, surely, must make them your original workaholics). They are both relatively short, but on stage their aura and charisma (a direct consequence of how they master bodily techniques) makes them larger than life. They are both generous artists, at the height of their relatively short careers, but they are also men of their time and generation, who grew up with Michael Jackson and Madonna as their icons.[26]

zero degrees, which results from this encounter, has an incubation period of more than three years, in which both protagonists grow toward each other and establish a strong friendship as a base for their artistic collaboration. When they enter the actual rehearsal process in the studios at Sadler's Wells in London in the spring of 2005, they have already clarified and defined the basic principles of their artistic journey together: they will exchange the knowledge of dance they have already accumulated individually, and they will each tell a story about their identity in-between cultures.

For Akram the story is an obvious one. He tells Larbi the story of a journey to India and Bangladesh and the questions it raises about his own 'foreignness.' Larbi records Akram telling the story and they both reenact the original rendering, copying all repetitions, hesitations, pauses, as well as the exact hand and head movements accompanying them. These hand movements have already become a signature part of Larbi's choreographic language. Referencing the ideas of his rhythm teacher Fernand Schirren,[27] Larbi considers the hand movements that accompany our talking as the 'origin' of choreography. Akram's Kathak work also places great importance on the use of the hands: they tell the stories of the Indian gods. The collaboration sparks Larbi's career-long interest and research into the use of the hands in different dance traditions. He will go on to work in, among others, flamenco in *Dunas* (2009), Kuchipudi in *Play* (2010), and tango in *Milonga* (2013).

'And what I remember, is...' Akram's narrative starts with a crossing of a border and him being asked to prove his identity—an identity that completely coincides with a document, his passport: 'Suddenly I realized how vulnerable I felt because if that passport disappears where is my proof of identity? They could just say I am Bangladeshi. I am a bandit. This was [...] It is amazing how much a passport holds, how much power a passport holds. A passport holds between a good life and a bad life, between life and death. I mean, it holds everything in just a piece of paper.'[28] In one of the opening chapters of *In Europe* (2004), Geert Mak describes how Stefan Zweig in 1915 could travel to India and America without owning a passport or 'ever having seen one.' One hundred years later, the passport has also become, even for the still-privileged European traveller, 'the most valuable book that he owns.'[29] It determines both your identity and your mobility.

As the train journey unfolds further, Akram discovers that he is a 'foreigner' in his country of 'origin.' He self-mockingly describes himself: 'It is really hot, and I just feel like, I just need to get to a hotel, cause [...] Initially we were gonna go to live with some friends. But I thought: no... I need my conveniences.

I need my essential supplies. And those were: a bathroom, a bath, a hot shower, erm, television, MTV, the usual things. The usual things that we are used to in the West.' A 'foreigner' who needs his cousin to explain the local customs to him and prevent him from getting into trouble because of his ignorance and his different way of behaving: 'It is not my clothing, I don't think. It is just my mannerisms. They can identify that I am a foreigner. And maybe it is arrogance.'[30]

Akram's narrative of his journey provides the ideal backbone for *zero degrees*. It is edited in four parts, which are spread across the entire length of the piece. The different movement sections, which all originate from a simple movement research idea that either Akram or Larbi has or which they share, organically find a connection with parts of this narrative. The hand movements accompanying the narrative are further explored in a movement sequence for hands and arms, in which both protagonists explore in a physical way how their identities mirror each other. This duet is followed by a second, which explores the turns (or *paltas*) of Kathak in a contemporary way and leads to a fight sequence and a first separation, allowing Akram to manipulate Larbi's body like a basketball. This then leads into Larbi's solo in which his dummy 'abuses' him.

The 'dummies,' as the artistic team fondly nickname them, are the main set design contribution by the British visual artist Antony Gormley, for whom *zero degrees* is his first stage design for a dance piece. In a similar way to how the casts of his own body have populated both urban and rural environments such as London, Crosby Beach in Liverpool, or the Swiss Alps, Gormley now makes plaster casts of both Akram and Larbi. They heighten the 'twin' motif of resemblance. But as puppets they also allow for an 'uncanny' treatment of these bodies, which wouldn't be possible with real bodies. Kenneth Gross, in his book *Puppet: An Essay on Uncanny Life* (2011), describes how doing what isn't possible with real bodies is one of the main functions of the puppet. The puppeteer Sue Buckmaster, too, who I interviewed as part of a *body:language* talk at Sadler's Wells in 2012, writes in her MA thesis 'A Psychoanalytical Study of the Power of the Puppet' that 'puppets have a subversive power to act out what we normally feel should be repressed behavior.' She goes on to say that 'their most subversive act is their ability to make us confront our acknowledgment of death.'[31] In the last days of the rehearsal process of *zero degrees*, we develop a number of short scenes with the dummies which come to play an important role as interludes, being subversive but also offering comic relief. An example is the scene where Larbi kicks Akram's dummy and Akram's body acts out the impact it receives.

All the movement sections eventually find a logical connection within the main narrative. The Shaolin moves, which originate in Akram's and Larbi's shared admiration for Bruce Lee, physicalize Akram's verbal fight with the border guards. The percussive Kathak footwork illustrates the relentless train journey. Two thirds into the narrative, the story shifts from its original question of identity to a story about a 'dead body on a train.' From there on, *zero degrees* becomes a contemporary lamentation for this dead body, performed in different languages and traditions. Akram retells the story using *abhinaya*, the storytelling element of Kathak. Larbi reenacts it in a comic farce with the dummies. Akram dances a contemporary solo around his dummy, becoming the 'aura' around his own dead body. Larbi sings the song that he has chosen as his original story, holding his dummy in a pietà-like manner.

This song, *Yerushalayim shel Zahav* [Jerusalem the Golden], is the semi-official anthem of the State of Israel and was originally sung by Naomi Shemer. It tells the story of a people in exile who eventually return to their home city. Larbi's choice of this song is inspired by a complex web of motives. By using a Yiddish song, he—as an 'Arab'—reaches out to the Other. 'We thought it would be interesting to use the voice of the other culture that is supposed to be our opposite in order to express a shared desire: to return home. To say it with the words of the one that is a stranger to us.'[32] But the song also illustrated his belief in the interrelatedness of all cultures and traditions, since he discovered that the Yiddish melody goes back to a Basque lullaby. Singing the song in a lamenting manner, mixing his voice with Sufi singer Faheem Mazhar, he also reaches out to and mourns his own dead father.

Already during the creation process of *zero degrees*, there is a sense of heightened expectation about the outcome. In my dialogue with Akram and Larbi, I feel the need to protect them from unrealistic expectations or hopes that together they will invent a new choreographic language. In the programme brochure I write:

By no means expect a new, perfect blend of two languages. Language does not evolve that way, neither bodily nor verbally. If it did, the result would be gobbledegook. Language evolves slowly, renews itself organically, soaks up elements from other languages, finds creative translations for 'foreign' elements. And the more two people understand and respect the other language and culture, the more effective and interesting the translation process.[33]

Even today, almost ten years after its creation, if you look at the video and have followed Akram's and Larbi's creative journeys, you can clearly identify each section with either one of them, or with both. Rather than try to blend and fuse their artistic identities, they choose—already in *zero degrees*—to juxtapose them, letting them coexist.

The headlines of announcements and reviews in the British press at the time of its premiere reflect both the expectations and the challenges of this collaborative exchange: 'A fusion of many worlds';[34] 'Opposites seek a seminal moment';[35] 'Marvelous hybrid kicks like a mule';[36] 'Two of a kind';[37] 'Opposites attract.'[38] Laurie Lewis in *The Independent on Sunday* effectively summarizes the pressures that these high expectations put on the actual production. She introduces her review with the statement that 'British-Bangladeshi Akram Khan is among the most charismatic dance talents in Britain. Flemish-Moroccan Sidi Larbi Cherkaoui holds a similar status in Europe. [...] Add a couple of more buzz names of the moment: sculptor Antony Gormley and composer Nitin Sawhney, and the project began to resemble a PR's fantasy wish list, all hype and hot air.' She continues, however: 'how good it is to be proved wrong. The overriding impression of *zero degrees*, [...] is of two deeply serious artists keen to address big issues on an intimate scale.'[39]

The initial reception is not unanimously positive. Some of the more conservative critics have problems with the meeting of Akram's 'classical Kathak' and Larbi's 'European tanztheater.' They stress the incompatibility of both dancers and regret not seeing a 'pure' movement-based dance without words or narrative. Strangely enough, very few reviews discuss the unexpected synchronicity that aligns the works with events in the real world: two young Europe-based choreographers with a Muslim background create a work lamenting 'a dead body on a train.' The piece's first public preview takes place on the day after the London metro bombings of 7/7, causing many 'dead bodies on trains.' Only the review in the *Metro* newspaper explicitly links both events: 'In the aftermath of last week's horrific events, there's a bleak temptation to read a post-apocalyptic message into almost everything. But there's no denying the timely resonance of *zero degrees*.[40] Maybe the other critics don't find it appropriate to make the link explicitly, but for the audience attending the first series of performances in London, the connection is obvious. The performances offer a release for their mourning, which in turn creates an emotional charge that stays alive until its final performances in New York three years later.

After their successful collaboration, both Akram and Larbi repeat the experience of working one-on-one with other artists. Akram creates *Sacred Monsters* with Sylvie Guillem and *in-i* (2008) with Juliette Binoche, both times repeating a similar compositional structure to *zero degrees*, that is, interweaving danced sections with narrative sections based on a shared theme. In *Sacred Monsters*, for instance, this shared theme is the experience of both protagonists having to live up to the expectations of being a 'star'—a 'sacred monster'—from a young age. The two different classical worlds that they both inhabited left very little freedom for self-exploration, which drove them toward contemporary dance: 'It is the dichotomy of the opposites. One place, which is the classical world, offers you tradition, history. It offers you discipline, something very sacred and spiritual, too. And the other place, the contemporary, offers you a science laboratory. It offers you your voice to be heard. It offers you numerous discoveries and possibilities.'[41] Larbi, on the other hand, engages in a series of duets in which he consciously seeks to study another dance language: Kuchipudi with Shantala Shivalingappa in *Play* (2010), and flamenco with María Pagés in *Dunas* (2009). In some of his ensemble pieces, too, he pursues his purpose of learning new dance languages, for example the language of Shaolin Kung Fu in *Sutra*, and tango in *Mįlonga*.

Lorna Sanders concludes her essay '"I Just Can't Wait to Get to the Hotel": *zero degrees*' (2005) with a series of questions that the performance raises: 'What is the source of identity? What can be shared with those from another culture, tradition or approach? How is your perspective shifted and our understanding altered? In what ways are we individual? In what qualities lies our humanity?'[42] Meanwhile Royona Mitra, focusing on the significance of *zero degrees* in Akram's artistic journey, defines it as 'a formal and narrative exploration of the politics of border spaces as a metaphor for the transient nature of diasporic identity.'[43]

However, the biggest compliment for an artist is when his or her work inspires another artist to create in their turn. In *On Beauty and Being Just* (1999), Elaine Scarry describes how beauty incites a forward movement in us that drives us to create ourselves. As such the practice of ekphrasis is the most positive feedback an artist can receive. *zero degrees* inspires the Indian poet Karthika Nair to compose a series of poems in which she poetically evokes the dialogue between Akram and Larbi and their reflections on their identity in-between. The sestina 'zero degrees: between boundaries' identifies the physiognomy of Akram and Larbi with the mythical figures of the warrior and the monk and rearticulates their journey across borders into the land of the dead.

> I leave thoughts on belonging, on being
> and the zeroth law that I willfully
> signed, and watch them — one compact, bordering
> short; the other pale and spare — vault streaked walls
> of culture and kinetic codes. Lock hands
> embrace dodge thrust. The duet/duel ends
>
> before I read which is which, if one's end
> spells start elsewhere. Threat and trust were being
> swirled in synchronised moves till just a hand
> was seen, a smudge. Then Warrior's great will
> and body juddered to a sudden crash; walled
> by a stillness that steals through any border.
>
> Monk departs, a worn being in his hands,
> crooning of a day when borders and walls
> will cease; midst white shells of spent words, I end.[44]

Myth (2007): Integrating Polarities

> One of the intentions of a mythological system is to present evocative images, images that touch and resonate in very deep centers of our impulse system, and then move us from these very deep centers into action.[45]

At first sight *Myth* (2007) doesn't deal with the notion of the identity of the migrant body in-between cultures, but it does research in an almost encyclopedic way how we build our identities from the complementary energetic polarities of our bodies. Sidi Larbi Cherkaoui's epic work *Myth* originally has a different title, *Traum*. 'How can a certain event mark an individual forever?, which the dancers summarize too quickly as: we work on traumas. To avoid this directness, the choreographer tempers his approach by saying: yes, but trauma is related in German to *Traum* and *Traum* also means dream.'[46] A trauma is a wound or scar which creates an energetic blockage, preventing our embodiment, the transformations necessary to realize the full potential of our body shape. Healing and unblocking always involves reliving the original traumatic experience, in order to become conscious of it and to create out of this consciousness a physical and emotional release. This process of reliving is slow, cyclical, and painful, because it happens mostly on the level of body tissue. 'People often think that after an injury, the body restores to its original state. But that is not so. The wound grows together, but with new tissue. The wound becomes a scar. It is like a butterfly, it becomes a new form. It is similar with a trauma: afterwards you have changed fundamentally.'[47]

I myself have several severe operations between the ages of two and five (one causing the need for another): a water cyst explodes in my belly, my intestines become blocked, and my throat is burnt without an anesthetic to stop its bleeding after the removal of my tonsils. In the sixth seven-year cycle of my life, between the ages of thirty-five and forty-two, after having started my yoga practice, I relive all this original pain in quite a literal way, knowing, however, that it is my body's memory of a past physical state and not an actual, present illness.

Often we need a catalyst to trigger this 'reliving.' It can be an accidental meeting with another person, another body, and the somatic transfer that takes place between both. Only a couple of days after writing these lines, I have another such experience of somatic transfer. I have just arrived in London and meet Kathelin, an American friend. We go for dinner and share our news since our last meeting a couple of months ago. During the conversation my body automatically tunes into hers. While walking to the restaurant my knee resonates with her recent knee injury. Later, different parts of my body which have recently been under pressure (the cortex, my eyes, my thumb), first experience some extra tension and then a release (at one point my eyes start watering without apparent reason). At the end of our dinner conversation, I suddenly feel very tired and need to go to bed early. As I wake up during the night, the process in my body which has been initiated by our meeting continues. The next morning I am completely revitalized. It is not the first time that this has happened. It has happened many times before, both in my private life (with people I have a close relationship with) and in my professional life (with some of the choreographers or dancers I have worked with). But it is maybe the first time that I am trying to articulate and communicate this experience to others. The process of 'remembering' can also become more ritualized. The origins of art, music, and dance in particular probably had this function: to offer to both the 'actors' and the 'viewers' 'evocative images' to trigger and relive somatic experiences. In *Myth & the Body: A Colloquy with Joseph Campbell* (1999), Stanley Keleman acknowledges how society uses 'song, dances and religious rituals to support these mythic images of the body and the experience it wishes people to have.'[48]

Sidi Larbi Cherkaoui's *Myth* also has the ambition to create such evocative images. Their list is long and expands at each viewing. Some are very specific: a howling woman being raped by a werewolf-man (or is he the embodiment of her own abundance of male energy?); the medieval iconography of vanitas depicted with a mirror and a skull, reminding us of the transitory nature of human life; a Christ-like figure carrying his cross and the burdens of humanity; Asian warriors, reminiscent of the Indian epics, fighting and killing each other in an infinite cycle of death and rebirth; Cerberus, the three-headed guardian of the underworld; a playful Peter Pan-like shadow, teasing the body it belongs to and escaping its control, and an Alice in Wonderland who grows and shrinks in unpredictable ways. Others are more generic: a spider-woman, a rejected child, a seamstress knitting a torn body, twins fighting and separating, a rejected lover, growling dogs.

In Jungian psychology these mythic images have an archetypical value and can be analyzed according to how they associate with each other, are repeated, or are amplified. Whereas instinct drives behaviour, the mythical archetype offers a model of perception and reflection to understand this behaviour. But it is a 'knowledge' that has to be thought in somatic ways, as centres of energy that condition, support, and orient the individual in his or her relationship with the environment. Daniel Sibony articulates this by defining the image 'not as a machine to look or to perceive but as a machine of transfer.' The image surfeits the immediate face-to-face situation and creates a transfer of 'memory-perceptions.' The memories invested in these images trigger other memories in the perceiver, which can result in an emotional identification and eventually also release and catharsis.[49] In Jungian psychology, some of the basic archetypes are anima and animus, the shadow, the child, the mother, the old wizard, and the hero.

While the company is performing *Myth* in Kalamata, Greece in the summer of 2008, I have one at least subjective confirmation that Sidi Larbi had been successful in his attempt to create evocative mythical images that can induce change in the spectator. A day after the performance, after an audience talk (which actually laid the foundation for this chapter), a Greek woman who has seen the performance comes to see me and tells me how she recognized in the performance, in quite a literal way, an image that has haunted her dreams for years. She hasn't dreamt about it recently, but in the previous night the image has returned to her dream differently from in past occurrences. She says that she feels it has been transformed.

Sidi Larbi Cherkaoui and I, as dramaturge, use the Tarot cards as a frame of reference for a symbolic and metaphorical language of mythic images. In *La Voie du Tarot* (2004), Alexander Jodorowsky describes how one of the possible origins of the Tarot cards lies in medieval Spain, where wise men from the three main Western religions, Christianity, Islam, and Judaism, shared their knowledge and mystic insights and recorded them in a kind of pictorial encyclopedia, whose underlying principles resemble the Eastern integration of complementary poles. Each individual figure or card includes in its multilayered uniqueness the knowledge and potentialities of all the others. Although they are numbered, there is no hierarchy between the cards, only a constant process of transformation from one to the other. The unity of the oppositions is organized around a vertical axis between heaven (the spiritual) and earth (the material), and a horizontal axis between a receptive (circular and more female) and active (square and more male) energy. 'As expressed in a Chinese proverb: the ideal is to be receptive to heaven and to be active on earth.'[50]

At the beginning of the creative process, Larbi draws a cartoon-like figure for each of the performers in his notebook, associating them with one of the Tarot's Major Arcana: 'Power,' for example, is a woman looking into the mouth of a lion. 'The World' is a Shiva-like dancer at the centre of the four basic energies, symbolized by an angel, an eagle, a horse, and a lion. Eventually Larbi lets go of this too simplistic identification between performer and archetypal character.

The open rehearsal process that he uses in his work stimulates and challenges his performers to explore and work with their own somatic experiences. As a result, the sources of inspiration and the starting points for choreographic research in *Myth* are extremely eclectic. Related to or brought to the table by the performers themselves, they exemplify the diversity of human characters and interests. 'With this project on archetypes, *Myth*, I need everybody, all typologies, all opinions, in a way that I can make any combination conceivable. You are able to recognize the essential—the four elements—in the characters because you have so many of them.'[51]

The dance skills of the performers, ranging from contortionist yoga flexibility, Eastern European folk dance and American tapdance to Asian martial arts, are explored, interchanged, and juxtaposed. For instance, in one section the rhythms of Darryl Woods's tapdance begin a dialogue with the folk dances of the Slovaks (Peter Jasko and Milan Herich), as well as with the 'Eastern' more fluid moves of Iris Bouche and Alexandra Gilbert, who both have a mixed, Eurasian background. The textual fragments in the performance are collected by the performers, taken from their lived experience, their reading, or from browsing the Internet: a conference paper by Jung about the Christ in each of us, a fragment of Peter Weiss's play *Marat/De Sade* (1964) on the animal nature in every man, Clarissa Pinkola-Estes's book *Women Who Run with Wolves* (1992), popular culture from different parts of the world such as the *Wizard of Oz* or Japanese Manga, an autobiographical text about the death of one's loved ones. The French writer Joël Kérouanton, who follows the creative process to translate it into his own fictionalized universe, also functions as a researcher, interviewing a French psychiatrist on trauma or adding some of his own stories, amongst others about an illegal immigrant neighbour being expatriated and deported.

Sidi Larbi Cherkaoui's rehearsal studio resembles a contemporary science lab where small groups of researchers autonomously research the same subjects from different angles. Yoga sessions in the morning and polyphonic singing at the end of the day keep the group together, 'in tune' which each other somatically. In *Pèlerinage sur soi* (2006), Larbi describes how the discovery of polyphonic singing through his dance partner Damien Jalet in his first production *Rien de Rien* (2000) was a real somatic experience and how since then, it has become an essential part of his own training and that of his dancers (together with yoga practice):

> I had never heard a similar thing before, and still I had the impression that it was anchored in my unconscious, written in my body. I was physically in resonance with this ancient music, it touched undeniably an element of my own biology. [...] What I appreciate in singing is that it is very concrete. There is no theory. You have to sing in order to sing. It is sufficient to do it in order to understand it. [...] Yoga and singing are two very concrete ways to learn about one's own body, one's strengths, limits and potentials.[52]

For Larbi, the challenge of such an open process is to bring all this individually generated material together to form a coherent universe. The notion of somatic and energetic opposites becomes the binding theme: how to reintegrate the shadow side, the animal in us. 'Opposites are the tensions that are part of the formative process. When we can embody these tensions, we form our individuality. We are all foolish and wise, wild and tame.'[53]

In *The Eye of Shiva: Eastern Mysticism and Science* (1980), Amaury De Riencourt also discusses how the East and West fundamentally differ in the way they deal with these 'pairs-of-opposites' around which our dualistic human existence is organized. For the Western mind opposites are antinomies. They imply opposition, incompatibility, an either/or relationship that can only be reconciled through a process of dialectic thinking. The Eastern mind considers binary terms as complementary, coexisting and even cooperating entities—as perfectly symbolized by the Chinese yin and yang alternation. What is more, these polarities are not considered static, fixed positions in which one lingers, but as dynamic energy fields through which one constantly moves. The characters in *Myth* are organized around such pairs of opposites, but they are never caught in black-or-white categorization and the different roles and typologies constantly shift and transform.

The scenography of *Myth* suggests a purgatory, a waiting room in-between. Like many of Sidi Larbi Cherkaoui's earlier works, it is defined by its walls. It is a *huis clos* [closed room] but this time, it also has one big gate. The whole development of the piece is built in anticipation of if and when this gate will open for the assembled people to move on, to be sent to heaven or hell in Christian mythology, to a doctor, or back into the world as in Eastern beliefs of reincarnation. 'We have been waiting here for a very, very long time.' From the very beginning, Woods's character sets the tone. He and all the other characters who have ended up in this in-between world either represent a pair of archetypal polarities and will have to confront their opposites in the course of the piece, or they embody their shadows or animal nature.

In an average full-length dance piece, there are between ten and twenty individually created sections. In *Myth*, there are more than fifty. It is a conscious choice by Larbi to be 'all-inclusive' and not to reject any of the images proposed by his dancers, to create a multilayered visual stream of (un)consciousness similar to that of dream associations in which it is both impossible to isolate an image or remember the whole. In order to manage this complexity, we organize the images into four distinct chapters, each introduced by a quote, as in a medieval emblem book:

> 'For those who know to wait, time opens its doors.'
>   (Chinese proverb)
> 'Oh vain shadows, except for their appearances.'
>   (Dante, Purgatorio, II, 79)
> 'Knowledge is always within the shadow of ignorance.'
>   (Krishnamurti)
> 'The sun has never seen a shadow.'
>   (Leonardo da Vinci).

Nevertheless, what these chapters mean exactly is never entirely fixed—it might be about the fear of the unknown or the other, the search for identity, the necessary process of separation, or healing. They constantly fluctuate and transform in a similar way to the characters who are also never just one-dimensional. Take for instance the 'mother' character played by Christine Leboutte.

In *Foi* (2003), the production that thematically precedes *Myth*, she remains within the register of the mourning mother looking for her lost son during the whole performance. In *Myth*, her character is still centralized around a basic sense of loss, but it is much more complex and she goes through very different, constantly shifting emotional states. In the beginning she is the survivor of a suicide attempt—ironically because her blood coagulated too quickly. She rejects a child being literally thrown out from between her legs, but toward the end of the performance she nurses another, discreetly in the background. She talks equally about an illegal immigrant neighbour being sent back, the animal nature of man, and her childhood fantasies relating to the death of her cat and her parents. She laughs hysterically, sings and howls, but she also tries to reassure the other 'lost souls' and comes to their defence when somebody is offensive towards them.

This multilayered complexity of the performer/character, in which very different personalities coexist, corresponds to our present-day reality of multiple identities and is another characteristic of Larbi's Eastern sensibility. 'Therefore, Eastern theatre forms interest me a lot, because the actor incarnates more than one character, both good and evil, man and woman. The actor is everything, everybody. One is capable of changing perspective all the time.'[54]

The inclusion in his choreographic universe of professional actors with Down's syndrome, whom he has met at Theater Stap when creating *Ook* (2002), is mainly inspired by their capacity to act with an unmediated physical directness, emotional empathy, and a resilience based on a somatic consciousness rather than a rational one. 'He [the actor Marc Wagemans] was verbally not very strong, but physically he remembered everything. [...] We judge people by the way they talk, but often there is as much meaning in the body. Words are often too weak to express what we think.'[55] In *Sidi Larbi Cherkaoui, Rencontres* (2004), Kérouantan describes in detail Cherkaoui's experiences with the actors of Theater Stap, how he discovers their professional talents when creating *Ook*, and how he invites two of them, Marc Wagemans and Ann Dockx, to be part of his own work *Foi* (2003) and *Myth*. For him it is another way of creating layers in the dialogue between self and other, between bodily and verbal knowledge.

There is one particular scene in *Myth* that stands out and that often makes the audience uncomfortable, as I experience myself during a post-performance talk in Ottawa. At the end of the second section, the black, male performer Woods launches an insulting rant against the actress with Down's syndrome, Dockx, who has consciously been dressed in bright white:

> Oh, so you think that you are all that? Doing your, Oh look at me, I am dressed all in white and I am blonde, blue eyed and innocent, vestal virgin, holier than thou. I am so good. I am a saint. Oooh, I am going to heaven act. Well, honey, if you are going to heaven, get me a first ticket to hell. Look at you, oh dear, did you let your husband dress you? You are always running around on your knees like you are a munchkin. Well honey you better ease on down the road, clasping your little bony, nubby, stubby sausage fingered hands together as if you are praying all the time trying to open the door to heaven. Honey, you are too short to reach the doorknob much less open the door. Well, I guess, if I looked like you, I would be praying too. Let me guess. You are the kid who made the silly face and it stayed that way. You are so ugly that when you look into the mirror your reflection throws up. If God made you in his image then he is damn ugly mother fucker too.[56]

The rant continues, using quotes from the popular MTV series *Yo Momma*, in which two people, often representing different social or ethnic communities, battle verbally, insulting each other's mothers. Throughout the rant, Dockx remains stoically unaffected. Eventually it is Woods himself who breaks down when he, and the audience with him, realize in front of a mirror that the hate directed toward the other has been in essence self-hate caused by his parents' non-acceptance of his own, gay identity. The stereotypical power relationships that have been established earlier in the scene between male and female, black and white, abled and disabled, completely crumble at the end when Dockx sings the Flemish traditional song *Ik zeg adieu* [I say farewell], showing that she understood from the very beginning the origin of his hatred and offering him her solidarity and consolation. 'Want waar gij zijt daar zal ik zijn/'t Zij vreugde of pijn [Wherever you are, I will be as well, in happiness or pain].'

In 'Dreams, Myth, History: Sidi Larbi Cherkaoui's Dramaturgies' (2011), her enlightening analysis of *Myth*, Lise

Uytterhoeven describes in detail a similar scene in which the Japanese performer Satoshi Kudo lends his voice to Wagemans in order to defend himself against the physical humiliations and verbal attacks of Ulrika Kinn Svensson. Kudo's 'emotional rant' is uttered in Japanese, 'in a military, almost propagandist way' without any translation, so that only a Japanese audience can understand that he is linking Hiroshima to the Gulf War and 9/11. Uytterhoeven concludes that 'this deliberate non-translation is characteristic of many of Cherkaoui's works, in which the performers often speak or sing in their various native languages. Cherkaoui can thus be seen not to favour Western languages, confronting the spectators with the limits to their own knowledge.'[57]

It is Sidi Larbi Cherkaoui's firm belief in the prevalence of somatic, experiential knowledge and the transformational nature of reality that also makes him distrust the written word as the main expression of Western rational thought and culture, at least when it tries to or pretends to fix reality into definite meaning. 'Once they are printed, words can't evolve anymore. I find this definite side of ink and paper intimidating. Every truth is related to a certain time. It is possible that the truth of what is written today becomes a lie of my future thoughts.'[58]

The background image of a book 'burning' in *Myth*, and the literal, physical weight of book knowledge under which the librarian character collapses, becomes the main theme of his next production, *Apocrifu* (2007). *Apocrifu* begins where *Myth* ends, with the questioning of the validity of the written word. In all ideologies and all religions, the written 'holy word' tends to become dogma, domesticating the human body and restricting free will. In a series of connected solos, *Apocrifu* shows how these mechanisms work. In the opening scene, the Japanese ballet dancer Yasuyuki Shuto, symbolizing man's striving upward toward heaven, descends a giant staircase like a bird caged by the weight of tradition, which is symbolized by the *ghungroos*, the traditional Indian anklet bells he is wearing. The French acrobat-dancer Dimitri Jourde follows with a more grounded, close-to-earth solo. Enters the choreographer, making a pathway for himself with books, connecting earth and sky. Later these books are violently thrown at each other. They blind or interrupt natural speech. They are identified with swords. In a monologue, taken from the Islamic scholar Jay Smith on YouTube,[59] Sidi Larbi Cherkaoui underlines the fact that the so-called 'holy word' is always a historical invention of man, and that different scriptures often go back to the same, apocryphal sources. In one of his signature choreographic sections, he and his two fellow dancers reenact Smith's words, illustrating how passages from the Koran (Surat 5 Ayat 31 and 32 on the story of Cain and Abel) and the Bible share the same sources. While reciting Smith's comments, they juggle with books like magicians, transforming their severe 'truths' into harmless objects to play with. A fourth character, a childsize puppet with which the choreographer identifies himself, tries to cut off its strings and eventually turns on its manipulators. When in his final solo the choreographer imitates the awkward movements of the puppet, before climbing the stairs once more, the final message seems to be that man should regain his autonomy, which fundamentally lies in the consciousness and control of one's own embodied incarnation.

With this finale of *Apocrifu,* Sidi Larbi Cherkaoui revisits the similar ending of *Myth.* When the gates finally open, a Christ-like figure (performed by Daniel Fournier) enters the stage, manipulating two wooden poles. Body and cross constantly shift: from a body hanging on the cross to a Saint Sebastian martyr figure being pierced by arrows to an upside-down Latin cross associated with Satanism. The scene is accompanied by the medieval song *Io sono un pellegrino,* evoking the figure of the pilgrim, the 'eternal wanderer.' At first all the other performers cling to the Christ figure, who has to push them away, echoing Jung on Christ, pointed to earlier. In it Jung instructs people to take responsibility for their own actions, saying that it is 'immoral to pass our sins on to Christ.' Eventually the Christ-like figure manages to push everybody to the other side of the gate, without revealing or resolving what is behind. Only Woods, who has been most impatient from the beginning, stays behind, dressed in white as a black, drag beauty queen. As the gate slowly closes again, a black Faith figure (Bouche) slips through, casting a last long shadow with her black robe. Black and white. The polarities have been kept intact and alive.

In parallel to the piece's visual dramaturgy there is a musical dramaturgy developed in close dialogue with Patrizia Bovi, whose Ensemble Micrologus—which specializes in medieval polyphonic music—provides live accompaniment. *Myth* opens with *Crucifixum in Carne* (Let us praise him who has been crucified in the flesh) and ends with *Sepulto Domino,* thus forming a musical arc from death to resurrection. *Myth* has an open ending and doesn't offer any solution. Uytterhoeven concludes her essay stating that the dramaturgies of *Myth* 'no longer privilege a single, unified (western) knowledge base and cannot be read without the spectator's active labor of decoding and understanding.'[60]

bahok (2008): One World, Many Languages

> It has long been a desire of mine to bring together artists from different cultures, who speak different languages, not only through their tongues but more importantly through their bodies.[61]

Leading up to the 2008 Summer Olympics in Beijing, the Akram Khan Company and the National Ballet of China broker a coproduction. In the beginning very little is defined for this production, except that Akram will involve some of the dancers he has worked with before and also integrate some of the Chinese ballet dancers which he will audition in Beijing. The rehearsal period is spread out over three months: a research month in London in the summer of 2007 and two months of creation in December 2007 in London and in January 2008 in Beijing leading up to a Chinese world premiere. When the nine dancers, with seven different nationalities (Chinese, Indian, Slovak, Spanish, South-African, South-Korean, and Taiwanese) meet for the first time in London, Akram is surprised by how little exchange and communication there is between them. He intuitively decides that this will be the main topic to explore. How will strangers who speak different languages and master different dance techniques (from ballet, folk dance, and martial arts to more contemporary idioms) relate to each other?

In the first four weeks of the research, the dancers take classes in each other's techniques. Akram also decides to focus less on the creation of movement material in the first improvisations, and instead to explore more theatrical exercises which are new and unknown to everybody. These exercises are inspired amongst others by a workshop he took with Simon McBurney, co-founder of Théâtre de Complicité. They include stories people have to tell about their dreams or about 'home,' and playing with everyday objects such as mobile phones or suitcases. The latter helps to define the environment and the theatrical setting of the piece: one of the faceless contemporary transit zones or non-places (such as for example airports or train stations), where total strangers end up sitting next to each other, obliged to interact.

Out of the stories, those about home turn out to be particularly powerful. To everyone's surprise, nobody talks about their present day home. Instead, everybody reminisces about the original childhood home that they grew up in, and about the strong memories that are associated with it. For Eulalia Ayguade Farro, for instance, it is the unique quality of the Spanish rain that represents home. This resonates with what Homi K. Bhabha writes, about the weather as one of 'the most changeable and immanent signs of national difference.'[62] For Shanell Winlock, from South Africa, home is the smell of burnt car tires in the townships, or of her father's shoes. Later in the process other stories are invented and added to the original ones, such as the story about the Indian temple being 'a place to train the senses' or the cliché of the 'spitting Chinese,' which comes about because of the daily commercials that the group watches on Chinese television during their final residence in Beijing, in which the local population is reminded to 'clean up' their behaviour for the foreign guests of the Olympics. In the final work some of these stories are told often in a performer's mother tongue, while others become the basis for one of the dance solos. The notion of 'home' being antithetical to the nomadic condition of the contemporary dancer also inspires the final title, *bahok*.

The story behind the name of a work often reveals how its content has shifted during the creation process. The first title we come up with for *bahok* is 'nomads,' highlighting the nomadic life of the contemporary dancer and using it as a metaphor for a more general, contemporary human condition. However, nomads already feels like too much of a cliché and has been used before, both for dance pieces and as a name for a dance company. For similar reasons we reject 'bridge.' During the first month of research, I am reading John Berger's collection of essays *Hold Everything Dear: Dispatches on Survival and Resistance* (2007), which includes amongst others an essay on the Palestinian diaspora. In this text, Berger states that, 'For nomads, home is not an address, home is what they carry with them.'[63] So I suggest to Akram the title 'carriers' instead of nomads, as it also addresses the body and its role as the main carrier of all the things we inherit and experience. Akram likes the new associations, but feels that 'carriers' lacks the necessary acoustic punch. Luckily, he has the idea to ask his mother to translate 'carrier' into Bangla, which results in the word 'bahok.' It combines the universality of the metaphor with the concreteness of the mother tongue. But the story of the name doesn't finish there. At its premiere in Beijing, the Chinese hosts decide, without informing anybody, to re-translate it into 相聚 [Getting Together]. While befitting the Olympic slogan of *One World, One Dream*, it means that the cultural specificity of the Bengali word is lost.

Parallel to these individual stories and from the first week of the rehearsal process on, Akram also starts to work on two larger dance sections with the whole group. But while in his early works the movement vocabulary was still very much Kathak-based, he now uses the diversity of the dancers' own dance techniques as his basis. Throughout the history of dance in the twentieth century, choreographers have tried to distinguish themselves from their predecessors and peers by developing their own signature movement vocabulary, often based on the idiosyncrasies of their own somatic identity. The passing on of this signature to other bodies has always been a complex, difficult, and slow process, in which the choreographer as a solo performer remained distinctive and set apart from the dancers who accompanied him. Only in the last decades of the twentieth century, under influence of choreographers such as Pina Bausch or Alain Platel, a new generation of choreographers has tried to create their own choreographic signature by building on the somatic identity of their dancers. Both Sidi Larbi Cherkaoui and Akram Khan are exemplary of this. In Akram's early group works such as *Rush* (2000) and *Kaash* (2002), the movement vocabulary is still very much developed in his own body and passed onto his dancers. Later, he allows his dancers to go through the same experiences that he has, that is, to imprint their contemporary bodies with Kathak classes, to let the technique absorb into their bodies and to let their bodies instinctively and somatically create a new identity out of this (the workshop model described earlier is an example of this process). In Akram's more recent productions, including *bahok*, the basis of the movement is owned by the individual dancers. He adds elements from his own technique and knowledge, such as the sense of rhythm or the 'illusion of speed.'

bahok begins with a long, silent scene, in which the dancers are simply waiting. Chairs and an old-fashioned analogue announcement board define the almost empty stage as a neutral transit zone. The board announces its messages with a soft clattering sound: 'Please Wait' or 'Delayed.' The first contact between Meng Ningning (from China) and Eulalia Ayguade Farro (from Spain) immediately sets the tone. Ningning addresses Farro with the limited words of English that both share, showing a desire to communicate but also its difficulties. To Ningning's question, 'Where does she come from?' Farro answers the obvious, 'I am not Chinese,' provoking immediate laughter in the audience. The fact that misunderstandings in intercultural dialogue often have a comic effect is used at several other moments in the performance: for instance in a danced duet in which Ningning tries to partner up with Indian dancer Saju Hari, matching her frivolous ballet moves and pirouettes to his more down to earth martial art technique of Kalaripayattu.

During the opening dialogue, the other dancers continue to wait and look for the next announcement while carrying the regular props of the contemporary traveller: bags, a suitcase, a newspaper, or a mobile phone. The use of these props in *bahok* resonates with Iain Chambers's discussion of how certain objects such as portable computers, mobile phones, and credit cards are 'privileged objects of contemporary nomadism'[64] which function as 'prosthetic extensions of mobile bodies caught up in a decentred diffusion of languages, experiences, identities, ideolects and histories.'[65]

The opening dialogue turns into a monologue in which Farro raises questions about her identity and origin, and, now addressing Hari, tells the story of how an Indian temple is designed to awaken the five senses and how this resembles her own experiences of the Catholic Church. But these superficial similarities also create confusion and Farro's coherence deteriorates more and more, expressing a sense of being lost. This introductory theatrical scene is followed by one of the two longer danced group sections in which each of the dancers presents his or her own particular movement language and technique, with the others forming a background chorus or sporadically joining in to create brief moments of synchronicity.

The production continues to interweave dance sections and theatrical interludes in a non-linear filmic way, zooming in and out between foreground and background. A dialogue between Winlock from South Africa and Kim Young Jin from South Korea depicts yet another situation of being 'lost in translation': together they are being interviewed by an invisible customs officer. The comic effect of the misunderstandings is tempered here; there is a more serious undertone and subtext since it is clear that misunderstandings can potentially influence whether one is allowed to enter the country or not. Their conversation finishes with Winlock admitting that she carries her father's shoes in her suitcase, which will be the theme of her dance solo later in the piece, and Young Jin telling a story in Korean, mixing his own childhood memories with the present reality of being in Beijing. The announcement board now functions as a translation device, but the subtitles reveal themselves as extremely limited in rendering the poetic and emotional qualities of the human voice articulating one's mother tongue.

At one point the communication problems and misunderstandings also lead to a verbal fight between Andrej Petrovič, a Slovak who is fed up with being identified as Russian, and Zhang Zhenzin from China. Kim Young has to mediate, silently, only using movement, but he gets stuck in the effort. Eventually everybody ends up in a group hug. Farro remains excluded from it until she crawls on top of all the others. When Hari's mobile phone rings again, the group breaks up and enters into the second long group dance. By this time everybody has become almost completely synchronous, in a rather mechanical and military way. During rehearsals this section was nicknamed the 'machine section.' Is this the 'One World, One Dream' that global capitalism wants to sell us?

A couple of days before the premiere, the Taiwanese dancer Sun Chia Ying has to return home for personal reasons. She has an important role in the production: among other things, her solo is conceived as the ending of the show. For a moment Akram considers replacing her with the understudy who has been accompanying the process, but Ying's movement language is too specific to be transferred to someone else at such short notice. Instead, we decide to reedit the whole piece, creating a new ending around Farro.[66] The original solo by Ying was based on a story of child abuse and had a much darker undertone, but now, through the 'accidents' of the creative process, the new ending has a more positive and hopeful message. Farro speaks to her mother on the phone (in her native tongue) while the announcement board starts having a life of itself, commenting on her. Farro becomes aware of this and eventually enters into a dialogue with the board, using the mobile phone as a remote control. At the premiere the announcements on the board read as follows:

Are you lost?
You look lost.
Do you know where you are going?
Is it in your papers?
Air
Water
Fire
Earth
But no address.
What are you carrying?
Body
Memories
Home
Hope
Home.[67]

Babel[words] (2010): Cacophony of Languages, Polyphony of Movements[68]

There are only two subjects in art: space and objects. The most potent and intelligent object that occupies space happens to be the human body.[69]

Antony Gormley creates a monumental and iconic set design for Babel[words]. During the entire performance, the dancers constantly manipulate the large aluminium cuboid frames in a playful game of deconstructing and reconstructing new spaces: a cityscape, a border control area at an airport, a boxing ring. Gormley has originally proposed this idea for zero degrees, where Larbi immediately likes it and has started to explore its creative potential. Akram, on the other hand is less convinced, prompting Gormley to propose another solution: a white cube stage and the 'dummies.' In the end it is a lucky decision, since clearly a larger group is needed to manipulate the large frames. But this anecdote illustrates very well Larbi's creative mind and process: never to let go of a fruitful idea and to re-appropriate and recycle it at the right moment. In a similar way he has been systematically expanding his dance vocabulary, studying and integrating different languages and techniques into his work. 'Larbi absorbs it, but then very quickly, and this is so extraordinary, he begins to mold it to his own purposes and sees how it might fit magnetically with something else, like that, with a chameleon-like ability to absorb the colors around him and then to begin to test them in new environments.'[70]

For *Babel*[(words)], Sidi Larbi Cherkaoui invites Jalet to co-direct and co-sign the work. Jalet has been an artistic partner since his first full length debut, *Rien de Rien* (2000) and he has been assisting and performing in many other creations, including *Foi, Tempus Fugit, In Memoriam, Loin, End, Myth, D'Avant, TeZukA,* and *Puz/zle*. It is a way for Larbi to acknowledge Jalet's importance as a partner and co-creator of his choreographic universe. They will continue this experience with the joint creation of *Boléro* for the Paris Opera Ballet.

'The first language humans used were gestures. There is nothing primitive about this language that floats from people's hands.'[71] *Babel*[(words)] starts with a monologue by Svensson. She recites an excerpt of Nicole Krauss's *The History of Love: A Novel* (2006), evoking a time before verbal language in which people communicated with gestures instead of words and in which they accepted the potential for misunderstandings. 'They didn't go around with the illusion that they could understand each other perfectly well. They were used to interrupt each other to ask if they understood correctly.'[72] Svensson is framed by a square of light and as she continues to speak, accompanying her words with a made-up sign language, the rest of the multi-ethnic cast forms a line behind her, squatting on the floor. The original cast consists of eighteen performers from thirteen different countries who among them speak fifteen different languages. As she steps aside, the first gesture they all make, one after the other, is to mark out their territory with their hands while calling out 'land' in their different mother tongues. The tone is set from the very beginning: language is strongly linked to territory, and misunderstandings and conflicts will arise from this association:

> Babel is about territory and language. How certain languages occupy a certain territory. And how, as humans, we always create a certain territory. We need a space around our body. All the other spaces are conventions between people. [...] What is inside? What is outside? Babel questions that these spatial conventions have an everlasting value. Like all conventions they are temporal. They change.[73]

Accompanied by a percussive rhythm, the dancers continue to mark the limited space around their bodies as they pass on certain movements, like domino blocks triggering each other. Living together is not only a matter of communication, but also and mainly about sharing physical spaces. As the intensity of the percussive music increases, the performers enact ritual fights and conflicts in the form of abstracted martial arts duets. The group forms various combinations, ranging from duets and trios to a sextet, and then back to quartets. At one point the imaginary territories are literally framed by Gormley's aluminum frames, defining different 'tribal' zones. Eventually everybody ends up in a small square in the middle of a larger configuration. The shared living space, a metaphor for our contemporary urban experience, is clearly too narrow and overcrowded. So people drop out again, one by one emptying the space until only the three main 'characters'—Leboutte, Svensson, and Woods—are left behind.

Woods, who is dressed as a posh real estate agent, gives a lecture and promotes the qualities of contemporary urban architecture while Leboutte, in a shaggy and old fashioned outfit, starts cleaning the aluminum frames in the background. The three characters are maintained throughout the piece. Later on, Woods will also lecture on mirror neurons as a possible explanation why we learn through imitation and why we develop empathy for others. The text of this monologue is a literal rendering, not only of the words but also of the gestures, of a TED talk by Vilayanur Ramachandran, a choreographic 'translation' device Larbi has used in a lot of his recent work. There will be a third monologue by Woods in which he ironically praises the unique qualities of English as the dominant language, seated on a throne created by the bodies of all the other dancers:

> English is the most widespread language in the world and is more widely spoken and written than any other language. [...] English is the medium for 80% of the information stored in the world's computers. [...] People who count English as their mother tongue make up less than 10% of the world's population, but they possess over 30% of the world's economic power. Therefore, in terms of quantity of transmitted information, English is the leader by far.[74]

Leboutte will continue to perform her role as the migrant cleaner, hanging up laundry between the frames and by doing so disturbing their clean look. In another scene, set at a border crossing, she is the only one who is subjected to a rigorous body check and eventually decides to stay behind. These theatrical scenes always have a strong comic effect. 'Babel surprises because it is so comic, but the comic also shows the desperate attempt to communicate and that we trust too much on words for this. And today these words don't function anymore and we have lost confidence in them.'[75]

In another comic scene, Svensson performs a human avatar, produced by IKEA and operated and manipulated by the Japanese performers Kazutomi Kozuki and Shogo Yoshii, who talk to each other in their mother tongue. All through the piece, everyone speaks their own mother tongue without any translation being offered. Uytterhoeven discusses in detail Cherkaoui's strategy of 'heteroglossia,' of letting different languages coexist on stage without offering the audience a full understanding. Reminiscent of my own discussion of translation theory,[76] Uytterhoeven refers to Lawrence Venuti's concept of 'foreignizing' which 'undermines the notion of fluency in translation which dominates the canons of accuracy' prevalent in a dominant language such as English.[77] Uytterhoeven concludes: 'As a postcolonial figure and a xenophile, Cherkaoui refuses to translate for the benefit of merely Western audiences. Alternative, postcolonial voices are embraced in his works, but the key to accessing their message is placed in the hands of the spectator. The absence of translation precisely highlights, firstly, the jarring need for translation and, secondly, the political problems of translation.'[78]

Positive images (for example a sensitive duet in which two dancers explore touching each other) and negative images (a dancer [Helder Seabra] fighting with capoeira moves against the virtual space he is imprisoned in) continue to alternate. Verbal cacophony alternates with tuned-in polyphonic singing and synchronized movement sections. The spaces defined both by Gormley's frames and the bodies manipulating them constantly transform until the final image, in which the dancers recreate their original line. This time, however, they are connected by their interlocking feet, so that they can only move together if they wait for and listen to each other, synchronizing their movements. They form a human chain connected to the earth. 'I have to adapt myself to the rest of the group. It slows me down and it is tiresome but it is also beautiful, like a wave that continues. If you feel yourself one with the other dancers, you have the patience to wait for the last person to join in.'[79] This final image recapitulates the experience the audience has had all through the performance: admiring the virtuosic collaboration and cooperation of a heterogeneous group of dancers, whether manipulating the frames or just walking as a crowd on stage. It is this pedestrian, somatic 'wisdom of the crowds' which is also described by James Surowiecki, that *Babel*(words) celebrates. A wisdom we all practice in our daily commutes through the cities we live in.

The critical acclaim for *Babel*(words) is exceptionally high. In London it receives two Laurence Olivier Awards for Best New Dance Production and for Outstanding Achievement in Dance (for its set design). In 2011 it also receives a Prix Benois de la Dance in Moscow. Judith Mackrell of *The Guardian* summarizes how it is received:

> Sidi Larbi Cherkaoui knows in his bones how deep the division of culture can go. His previous works *Foi* and *Myth* were both inspired, if ultimately unhinged by the vastness of that subject. But in *Babel*, which completes the trilogy, Cherkaoui and his co-choreographer Damien Jalet contain their material within the most fiercely resonant dance theatre of the decade. [...] Even within the fractious world that *Babel* presents, the cast seem drawn to sing and dance with each other. And it is a tribute to the work's knife-edge precision that it contains optimism and despair in such brilliantly equal measure.[80]

Desh (2011): Dialogue with the Homeland

> Akram, go back to yourself, to your origins: find what is in your body. So much of your self has been shared with others these last years. It is time to find something that is inherently yours. Uncalculated, dreamlike—like a conversation with a river. Or yourself.[81]

There is really no secret about how to reach artistic results of high quality. You always get back what you invest and in the performing arts that is mainly time and the human resources involved. I know few dance projects which have been so well prepared and in which all the artistic collaborators have been so invested as *Desh* (2011), Akram Khan's solo performance about his relationship with Bangladesh, his parents' home country. The Bangla word 'desh' has multiple meanings. It can equally mean 'land,' 'nation,' 'region,' or 'soil.' In *Desh*, Akram Khan reconnects with his heritage, both its physical reality and its (hi)stories.

He surrounds himself with an exceptional team of collaborators: dramaturge Ruth Little and lighting designer Michael Hulls (both of whom he has already collaborated with), set designer Tim Yip, composer Jocelyn Pook, as well as poet Karthika Nair and spoken word artist Polarbear who write the 'stories' on which the narrative is based. Together they invest in an intensive research process that is spread out over almost a year. At one point they all travel to Bangladesh together and immerse themselves in what Richard Sennett describes as the 'anthropological identity' of a nation: its sounds, smells, and tastes; its customs and collective stories. They embark on a creative journey, interweaving their different artistic voices and disciplines.

Katalin Trencsényi's book *Dramaturgy in the Making* (2015) includes a chapter on dance dramaturgy in which she speaks in detail with Little about the intensive research process that initiated *Desh*. 'Following the embodied research, the creative team of *Desh* made a trip to Bangladesh. "We said we have to go and live, smell, eat, drink and sleep Bangladesh," Akram Khan recalls of the team's desire to make a physical connection with the country during their research.'[82] Little even learns Bangla in preparation of their trip.

The documentary film *The Six Seasons* (2012), which Gilles Delmas makes about the creation process of *Desh*, clearly shows how the concrete experiences and impressions are translated in the final result. Hulls takes his inspiration for the lighting design from the omnipresent water and rivers. Pook weaves not only her field recordings of the diverse local music traditions but also the dense noises of traffic and working bodies that they encounter everywhere into her compositions. For Yip, some of the main sources for his set design are the threads and the incredible naturally dyed colours of the weavers. Akram himself remains at the centre of all this—it is his body that will eventually embody all the impressions and characters that have left a mark on them. The opening sequence of the piece, for instance, is clearly inspired by the ship breakers who dismantle huge cargo ships with nothing but hammers and their bare hands.

The Six Seasons moves forward and backward between the travel images of Bangladesh and the stage of the MC2 theatre in

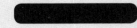

Grenoble where Akram is artist in residence and where much of the movement research takes place. For this research, Akram invites befriended choreographers and dancers to offer him ideas, including Jalet, Samuel Lefevre, Andrei Nazarenko, Jozef Frucek, and his rehearsal director Jose Agudo. It is for instance Jalet who comes up with the idea that the back of Akram's bald scalp also resembles a face, and that he can draw one on it, creating yet another character: a cook in a Bengali village, an alter ego of his father.

During the research process, different characters are explored and defined in close dialogue with poet Karthika Nair. She introduces Akram to the historical figure of Noor Hossain, a Bangladeshi youth party leader who was shot dead during a protest march against the military dictatorship in 1987, having written 'Free Democracy' and 'Down with tyranny' on his naked torso. 'We really cannot avoid political issues in *Desh*, that would mean denying this country its heartbeat.'[83] It feels like a significant coincidence that the friend who helped Hossain to write the slogans on his body was also called Akram.

The girl Jui is another character that Akram will bring alive. On one of their field trips the photographer and political activist Shahidul Alam brings them to the Jumma, a suppressed minority living in the mountains where the children are hired by Microsoft to test run and debug new software, a task that valorizes them and gives them a real sense of autonomy in a country where their own government is trying to suppress them. In the same way that Akram develops sketches of movement ideas, Nair writes sketches of possible texts and dialogues:

> There's this guy calling our Tech Support hotline these days. He doesn't know nuts about configuring the planner on his phone and claims that's totally messed up his life. He introduced himself as British-Bangladeshi, so I said I was Bangladeshi too. He suddenly went ballistic about syncing. Yelled and swore and said do you know who I am? I am world famous. I dance at the Sydney Opera House. Who cares? It's not like he's Lady Gaga![84]

During the whole creation process these sketches are revisited and rewritten over and over again to find their essence and necessity within the overall story, and also to find the proper form to express them. Trencsényi quotes Little comparing Akram's working process to 'a rocket ship's journey: as it travels further, it gradually sheds the unnecessary pieces, until only the engine capsule remains, containing the essential parts.' Little also describes how she is 'watchful that the text doesn't become an apology for movements.'[85] A lot of the rewriting process is about erasing or replacing the text with images or movements.

Nair writes a long ecologically inspired children's story about a boy stealing honey from the bumblebees and being punished for it by a Bengal tiger. From early on in the research process the artistic team decides to keep only the introductory sequence in which Akram tells this story to his fictional niece Eeshita in order to trick her into learning Bangla. For the rest of the story Akram switches to *abhinaya*, the Kathak way of telling stories with movements, while digital animation creates the environment and the other characters of the story.[86] 'It all started with Akram wanting to bring the question of transmission in *Desh*. To capture the sense of futility felt by grandparents and parents at their children's rejection of things that they had fought for: in this case, Bangla.'[87] All through the performance Akram will switch smoothly between English and Bangla, which remains untranslated.

In the end, what binds all these stories and characters together is Akram's own relationship with them: in particular how his relationship with Bangladesh is so different from that of his parents, most importantly his father's. The father-son relationship is at the core of the work. It illustrates how the father tries to share and even push his memories on the son, how the son rejects them because they are not his, and how he has to look for his own experiences. At the same time, even this, the backbone of the narrative, transforms in the course of the creation process. Little gives another good example of this; originally Akram himself wrote a detailed autobiographical monologue of his experience of having to work in his father's restaurant and his sense of being lost and torn between the loud, demanding customers. In the final staging this essential and well-written text was 'shed in order to integrate into the movement the memories and feelings it helped to bring out.'[88] His teenage memory also merges with a more recent one: the dense traffic in Dhaka, Bangladesh's capital, which is evoked on stage through the lighting design and soundscape.

Another personal story that has a prominent place is the family story of Akram's uncle who was part of the guerrilla force fighting for Bangladesh's independence and who saw a friend being captured and the soles of his feet sliced off. In *Akram Khan: Homeland, the Making of Desh* (2011), another documentary about the creation process, Akram identifies with this story from his experience as a dancer, whose 'hands and feet are the windows of the soul to connect to the soil and the sky.' 'The deadpan horror of this last event is seared into the mind when he enacts the aftermath by dancing on every surface of his body except the soles of his feet.'[89] Earth and sky and ecological references are an important subtext in *Desh*. All through the work a tension is created between the horizontal and vertical dimensions of life and experience. In the opening scene, Akram moves close to the floor and is eventually pulled upward when the backdrop rises. Later in the piece, he evokes another story told by his father about the long tall grass at home that looks as if it is growing out of the sky. In the finale, Yip lowers thousands of golden ribbons and Akram is pulled up in the midst of them, hanging upside down. The ecological theme reminds us of the climatological and ecological vulnerability of Bangladesh, the country with six seasons.

Similar to *Babel*[(words)], *Desh* receives a Laurence Olivier Award for Best New Dance Production and the TMA Award UK for Achievement in Dance in 2012. The British reviews after its UK premiere at the Curve Theatre in Leicester all acknowledge that the theme of identity is at the core of *Desh*. 'With *Desh*, Khan returns to the theme of identity, a major strand in his work, with new depth and immediacy';[90] 'His new solo *Desh* is a substantial work, some 90 thoroughbred minutes of episodic dance, dialogue and drama that tells of home and identity';[91] 'Khan has explored this cultural interzone before, sifting its misunderstandings and highlighting its exhilarating new forms';[92] 'It is essentially a journey. Khan was born in London, of Bangladeshi descent and *Desh* is his attempt to understand his parents' country and thereby make sense of himself';[93] 'What emerges from this material is both a sense of what it means to claim a cross-cultural identity, as can Khan, and to be a citizen of Bangladesh in the 21st century';[94] 'The ever-present tensions between history and identity, the collective past and the personal present; the paradoxical state of being that is the condition of the second-generation immigrant';[95] and 'Beginning with the startling image of him bashing a sledgehammer into a small, grave-like mound, it blossoms into a vivid, humane and amazingly accessible exploration of his past, his family and his cultural roots.'[96]

In *Desh*, Akram Khan intermingles personal memories and stories borrowed from Bangladesh's national history. It is this internalization of personal and political history, of his own and other people's traumas and heritage that allows Akram to go beyond his own persona. His body, his stories (real and borrowed) become the prism for a nation and put the contemporary history of Bangladesh at the core of a major British dance production. *Desh* is truly contemporary Kathak in the way it actualizes how the Kathak dancer embodies different characters and interweaves their stories.

Putting a New Social Imagery of the Migrating Body Centre Stage

Both *Desh* and *Babel*[(words)], show a high level of artistry and craftsmanship, interweaving different dance cultures and stage languages, but they also surprise by remaining extremely accessible. Sidi Larbi Cherkaoui and Akram Khan consciously aspire to and look for this accessibility. 'My work has become more and more accessible, even popular. [...] I don't want to address only an elite. I want to open doors.'[97] They thus not only receive high critical acclaim and an avalanche of professional prizes, but also attract large and diverse audiences.

By placing their work centre stage in the contemporary dance world not only in Europe but all over the world, they are creating a new social imagery on and about the migrating body. There are similarities in their specific 'stories,' but they are also fundamentally different and unique. Sidi Larbi Cherkaoui growing up in-between the different cultures of his parents has from the very beginning of his artistic career rejected any hierarchy between cultures and dance and music languages. He has set out on a journey to learn as many of them as possible, absorbing them and letting them coexist both in his own body and in the different bodies that cohabit his choreographic universes. The images he creates from these somatic experiences don't erase existing polarities but accept them and by doing so also transcend them. Sidi Larbi Cherkaoui shows how different dance and music cultures are interrelated and how the borders between them have always been permeable. He doesn't avoid showing the difficulties, the misunderstandings, and even the conflicts of an intercultural exchange, but also highlights the potential of dialogue and tuning-in polyphonically and somatically.

Akram Khan's artistic negotiation has been between the more homogenous Bangladeshi home culture of his parents and the Western European, British host culture in which it has been embedded. His strategy has been to use the confusion that resulted from this negotiation in a creative way: again both on the level of his own body and in the interweaving of both cultures on stage. He has placed his own culture and languages (Kathak and Bangla) and their themes centre stage in the contemporary British and European world of dance and performance.

Both Sidi Larbi Cherkaoui and Akram Khan allow different verbal languages (European and non-European) to coexist on stage without being translated, often showing the limits of what translation can actually achieve. The different dance and music languages don't fuse or blend into something new either, but are juxtaposed. What is shown is the possibility of dialogue between them, stressing the uniqueness of each language and of each embodied experience and story. As such they concretely oppose and undermine the cliché of a universal and generic dance culture.

Sidi Larbi Cherkaoui and Akram Khan also reject some of the obvious categorizations or labels that they might fall under, such as 'South-Asian' or '(post-)migrant.' At the same time, they have been using their identity in-between cultures strategically to create for themselves a place in the landscape of contemporary performance. How both have capitalized on the symbolic value of their identity to gain support and a secure position in the political and economic sense would be a rich subject for yet another study. For now it will suffice to mention how regularly they are presented in the media as role models and how they are institutionally recognized for this. Sidi Larbi Cherkaoui received amongst others the Kairos Prize for artistic vision and cultural dialogue (2009), the Flemish Cultural Award for the Performing Arts (2012), a nomination for European Cultural Ambassador (2013), the title of Young Artist for Intercultural Dialogue between Arab and Western Worlds from Unesco (2011), Commander of the Order of Arts and Letters of France (2013), and Maestro Honoris Causa from the Antwerp Conservatory (2013). Akram Khan received an MBE for services to dance (2005) and honorary doctorates and fellowships 'in recognition of outstanding efforts and unique contributions to the arts' from De Montfort University (2004), Roehampton University (2010), and Trinity Laban Conservatoire for Music and Dance (2010).

Sidi Larbi Cherkaoui's and Akram Khan's work gives a possible answer to Rosi Braidotti's plead for a new social imagery which is both embedded in a concrete narrative and embodied in a lived, somatic experience. This new social imagery, created by 'migrants' of the second generation, redefines the European identity as both becoming minoritarian and nomadic.

Notes

1 Sidi Larbi Cherkaoui in Jans 2009, p. 119.
2 Cité nationale de l'histoire de l'immi-gration which, ironically, is housed in the converted former Palais des Colonies.
3 Cherkaoui 2007, pp. 9-10.
4 Cherkaoui 2007, pp. 13-14.
5 Cherkaoui 2007, p. 19.
6 Cherkaoui in Cools 2006b, p. 42.
7 Dunberry and Diaz de Garaio Esnaola are both founding members of the company Sasha Waltz and Guests, which comes on board to produce this work.
8 Cherkaoui 2006b, p. 37.
9 Sidi Larbi Cherkaoui in Cools 2014c, p. 9.
10 Thich Nhat Hanh 2001, p. 161.
11 Fakhr in Wiegand 2008.
12 Through Sri Pratap Pawar, Akram Khan's dance lineage goes back to the Maharaj family of Kathak dancers and the so-called Lucknow School. For more details, see Sanders 2004, p. 28.
13 Lopez y Royo 2003, p. 5 as quoted by Ananya Chatterjea 2009, p. 120.
14 Chatterjea 2009, p. 133.
15 Ibid., pp. 120-121.
16 It is also Burrows who first introduced me to the work of Akram Khan, when I was still the dance curator at Arts Center Vooruit in Ghent. I presented a mixed bill of *Loose in Flight*, *Fix*, and another Kathak solo as part of a focus on British dance, Dance UK 4 (2000).
17 See also Sanders 2004.
18 Sanders 2004, p. 7.
19 A different reading of this innovation would be the 'cleansing' which is al-ready mentioned above.
20 Chaudhry in Shah 2010, p. 2.
21 *Kaash* has been recently (2015) recreated for a new cast.
22 Sanders 2004, p. 7. The politics of labelling remain complex and ambiguous. In her recently published monography on Akram Khan, Royona Mitra (2015) rejects the term 'contem-porary Kathak' identifying the qualification 'contemporary' as a form of 'westernisation' of the non-Western dance form. As I already indicated in chapter 2, I consider and use 'con-temporary' in a more generic way, that is whatever is relevant here and now. As such Akram Khan is able to create a dance universe, based on the principles of Kathak that is contemporary.

23 Akram Khan in Cools 2012b, pp. 15-16.
24 From the press announcement on the website of the Akram Khan Company. Accessed May 2015. www.akramkhancompany.net.
25 Nair 2009, p. 5.
26 Cools 2005.
27 Fernand Schirren was originally rhythm teacher at Mudra, the school Béjart founded in Brussels, and then also took up the same position at PARTS, Anne Teresa De Keersmaeker's revival and reinterpreta-tion of Béjart's model. He taught there until his death in 2001. Counterdanse published Schirren's rhythm ideas in the book, *Le rythme primordial et souverain* (1996).
28 Performance text *zero degrees*.
29 Rushdie 2003, p. 427.
30 Performance text *zero degrees*.
31 Buckmaster 1997, p. 27.
32 Cherkaoui 2006b, p. 53.
33 Cools 2005.
34 Ghose 2005.
35 Frater 2005.
36 Brown 2005.
37 Dougil 2005.
38 Mackrell 2005.
39 Gilbert 2005.
40 *Metro*.
41 Akram Khan in the program brochure of *Sacred Monsters*.
42 Sanders 2005.
43 Mitra 2010, p. 40.
44 Published in amongst others: Jeet Thayil, ed., *The Bloodaxe Book of Contemporary Indian Poets* (Tarset: Bloodaxe, 2008), p. 315 and in Karthika Nair, *bearings* (Noida, IND: HarperCollins India, 2009), pp. 5-6.
45 Keleman 1999, p. 34.
46 Kérouanton 2007, p. 176.
47 Cherkaoui 2006c, p. 4.
48 Keleman 1999, p. 35.
49 Sibony 1991, p. 269.
50 Jodorowsky 2004, p. 82.
51 Cherkaoui in Cools 2007, p. 119.
52 Cherkaoui 2006b, pp. 30-32.
53 Keleman 1999, p. 64.
54 Cherkaoui 2006c, p. 50.
55 Cherkaoui in Kérouantan 2004, p. 51.
56 Performance text *Myth*.
57 Uytterhoeven 2011, p. 338.
58 Cherkaoui 2006b, p. 10.
59 Jay Smith, 'Is the Qur'an the Word of God?,' debate connected to the Hyde Park Christian Fellowship, Southbank University, London, 29 May 1996. http://debate.org.uk/topics/history/debate/debate.htm. Accessed May 2015.

60 Uytterhoeven 2011, p. 339.
61 Personal e-mail from Akram Khan to the artistic collaborators of *bahok*, 18 April 2007.
62 Bhabha 1994, p. 243.
63 Berger 2007, p. 129.
64 Chambers 1994, p. 50.
65 Ibid., p. 52.
66 This editing process will go on after the premiere and *bahok* will only find its definite shape and structure on tour. My description here is based on the original version in Beijing and as registered during the ImPulsTanz Festival in Vienna in 2008. In later versions Eulalia's opening monologue will be presented later on in the performance, which starts directly with the long group dance section.
67 Performance text *bahok*.
68 I didn't work as a dramaturge on *Babel^(words)*, so my perspective here is different from the other works I discuss: mainly that of a spectator.
69 Gormley in *The Independent*, 22 April 2004.
70 Gormley in the Goudvis Documentary, *Sidi Larbi Cherkaoui: alle dansers zijn migranten*, 2011.
71 Performance text *Babel^(words)*.
72 Ibid.
73 Cherkaoui in the Goudvis Documentary, *Sidi Larbi Cherkaoui: alle dansers zijn migranten*, 2011.
74 Performance text *Babel^(words)*.
75 Brigitte Furle, intendant of Berliner Festspiele in the Goudvis Documentary, *Sidi Larbi Cherkaoui: alle dansers zijn migranten*, 2011.
76 See also Cools 2000.
77 Uytterhoeven 2013, p. 180.
78 Ibid., p. 184.
79 Sidi Larbi Cherkaoui in the Goudvis Documentary, *Sidi Larbi Cherkaoui: alle dansers zijn migranten*, 2011.
80 Mackrell 2010.
81 Tim Yip in Nair 2013, p. 17.
82 Trencsényi 2015, p. 236.
83 Nair 2013, p. 18.
84 From Nair's personal notes.
85 Trencsényi 2015, pp. 230–231.
86 Karthika Nair's original story, *The Honey Hunter* has meanwhile been successfully published in several languages. This particular story has also opened up the possibility for a children's version of *Desh*: *Chotto Desh* which will be created by theatre director and puppeteer Sue Buckmaster (Theatre Rites) in 2015.
87 Nair 2013, p. 37.
88 Trencsényi 2015, p. 238.
89 Norman 2011.
90 Anderson 2011.
91 Frater 2011.
92 Jennings 2011.
93 Monahan 2011.
94 Hutera 2011.
95 Sulcas 2011.
96 Norman 2011.
97 Sidi Larbi Cherkaoui in Boisseau 2013, p. 44.

Coda: The In-between of a Dialogical Art Practice

Clearly, a refusal of the destiny of the West need not simply imply a slide into historical oblivion and cultural suicide. Rather than seeking to speak on every occasion and in every location (in the name of science, rationalism, technology and knowledge), it is perhaps also necessary to acquire the habits of listening: to open up our language, our domesticating principles, to the unforeseen consequences of conversation, dialogue, even incomprehension.[1]

The Rebirth of Dialogue: The Art of Listening

If we were apprentices of listening rather than masters of discourse we might perhaps promote a different sort of coexistence among humans: not so much in the form of a utopian ideal but rather as an incipient philosophical solidarity capable of envisaging the common destiny of the species.[2]

Since Mikhail Bakhtin, there has been a reevaluation and reorientation of the importance of dialogue within the classical rhetorical tradition since Socrates and Plato. In *The Rebirth of Dialogue: Bakhtin, Socrates, and the Rhetorical Tradition* (2004), James P. Zappen gives an overview of how 'the emergence of dialogue as a response to cultural values embedded within printed texts, beginning as early as Bakthin and extending to recent discussion of the new digital media'[3] mirrors the way in which Socratic dialogue had been a response to an older, oral tradition. Zappen's book analyzes in detail how Bakhtin returns to the early Platonic dialogues in which 'a change, and exchange, of speaking subjects' rather than 'a single speaker' creates 'a collision of voices by which old ideas are challenged and new ideas are born.'[4] Bakhtin's concept of dialogue gives priority to the 'utterance in context' as opposed to the 'written sentence' (similar to the emergence of speech act theory as opposed to more traditional linguistics). Dialogue always implies a relationship with the larger context:

Unlike the sentence [...], an utterance exists only in context: it is spoken by someone, in response to something, in anticipation of a response from someone else. It thus exists not in isolation but only in relation to other utterances—in an exchange of utterances. The utterance therefore requires the active understanding of the listener, who must grasp the utterance and prepare to respond to it, who thus participates in shaping the utterance as it is being made (not after it is made).[5]

In order for dialogue—as an exchange of utterances—not to become a cacophony, each participant in the dialogue also has to practice 'an active viewing of each utterance from the perspective of the other.' The dialogue is opposed to a monologic rhetoric. It proposes 'openness and incompleteness, becoming rather than being, the created rather than the given, the unfinished rather than the finished.'[6] This form of dialogue also clearly distinguishes itself from the dialectic. Its purpose is not to persuade the other but to let new ideas emerge out of a creative interaction between many voices.

Bakhtin developed his theory mainly for the analysis of literature (Dostoevsky, Rabelais), that is, for written texts, and as such it was picked up amongst others by Julia Kristeva to develop her concept of intertextuality. It is only in more recent writings such as by David Abram that the act of writing itself is questioned and that dialogical practice is seen to imply a renewed emphasis on oral culture and transmission. In *The Spell of the Sensuous* (1996), Abram argues amongst other things that we have lost our connection to the larger ecological environment, and the use of our own body as the memory bank of that connection, due to the overdevelopment of a written culture. The alphabetization and phonotization of language and writing, which replaced older pictographic systems in the Judeo-Greek tradition, have distanced language further from the phenomenological reality to which it refers.

Abram gives a detailed overview and critique of this evolution, referring amongst others to the legend of the Egyptian King Thamus, as recorded in Plato's *Phaedrus*. Thamus is supposed to have refused the gift of writing offered to him by the god Thoth, arguing that writing also induces forgetfulness, since we no longer need to remember from within ourselves, but can do so 'by means of external marks.' Further, writing also opens the door for misunderstandings and misinterpretations and as such doesn't bring wisdom but the 'conceit of wisdom.'[7] As a counter-strategy to this distancing, Abram pleads for a revalorization of oral cultures. The oral culture also always establishes a 'synaesthetic association of visible topology with auditory recall—intertwining of earthly place with linguistic memory,' which again is 'radically transformed by alphabetic writing.'[8] Abram concludes that the Jewish experience of 'exile' is also one by which alphabetic writing 'engages our senses in such a way that they provisionally sever from participating with the larger environment they are part of.'[9] But he also describes how in the Jewish tradition there has always been a counter-current of an 'Oral Torah,' which has recorded consecutive oral commentaries and interpretations in successive layers around the primary one, the Mishnah. 'Thus, in its visible arrangement the Talmud displays a sense of the written text not as a definitive and finished object but as an organic, open-ended process to be entered into, an evolving being to be confronted and engaged.'[10]

Gemma Corradi Fiumara is a contemporary philosopher who looks at the same Socratic tradition as Zappen but through the lenses of such twentieth-century philosophers as Wittgenstein, Heidegger, and Gadamer. In *The Other Side of Language: A Philosphy of Listening* (1990), she pleads for a reappraisal of the receptive act of listening within a dialogical practice. Fiumara opens her book with the observation that in the history of Western thought, 'logos' is mainly aimed at 'saying,' which is often the equivalent of 'defining'[11] and has no 'recognisable references to the notion and capacity of listening.'[12] This lack of a practice of listening, according to Fiumara, is also responsible for the growing subdivision and fragmentation of our knowledge. As we institutionalize we tend to listen to and support only our own areas of interest and lose the ability to listen to the larger frames of life.

> By its very nature, a non-listening language sustains the tendency to institutionalize a mutual suspicion between areas of research, an attitude possibly conducive to an increasingly rigid and drastic subdivision of responsibilities. Furthermore, in accordance with such an 'urge' to subdivide into categories, all sense of responsibility with the life of (and on) the earth ends up by being banned.[13]

For her, the lack of listening has severe ecological consequences, but it is also discernible in education and in philosophy itself, where the 'metaphor of "battle" is considered of greater value than, for instance, those of "gardening or choreography."'[14] Taking up

Gadamer's statement that 'to listen is to be fundamentally open,'[15] Fiumara continues to argue that listening is the precondition of creative thinking itself.

> If we cannot listen properly, it seems that we can no longer share "in creative thinking", and that we must confine ourselves more and more to circulating within a given repertory, or arsenal, of terms and standard articulations, which can be summoned up each time in mnemonic fashion: almost a pledge to comply with standard ways of mirroring and with reproductive thinking.[16]

Richard Sennett, in *Together: The Rituals, Pleasures and Politics of Cooperation* (2012), develops a similar argument to Fiumara and discusses how the lack of dialogical practice and the failure to exercise one's listening skills is one of the main reasons for diminishing social cohesion in the workplace.

> De-skilling is occurring in the social realm in equal measure: people are losing the skills to deal with the intractable differences as material inequality isolates them, short-term labour makes their social contacts more superficial and activates anxiety about the Other. We are losing the skills of cooperation needed to make a complex society work.[17]

As a sociologist, Sennett has been conducting extensive research on both the working conditions of back-office workers on Wall Street and those of computer programmers in Silicon Valley. His research provides both quantitative and qualitative data about how a short-term perspective has taken over on all levels of work, and how 'stability in the work has become a stigma' with 'project labour acting as an acid solvent, eating away at authority, trust and cooperation.'[18] Sennett describes several new pathologies such as anxiety and withdrawal, either into narcissism or complacency, which arise as a result of this process.

Sennett not only criticizes, but also tries to offer a vision and strategies for reversing or transforming the current state of affairs. One of the main strategies he proposes, besides revaluing rituals, is to practice dialogic skills such as 'listening well,' 'managing disagreement,' or 'behaving tactfully.' He also underlines the importance of recognizing the listener's share in a discussion, realizing that receptivity means paying attention to both verbal and non-verbal concrete details in order to understand not only what is said but the underlying assumptions as well. He also refers to Bakhtin's notion of the dialogue as an open, never finished process and thus distinguishes it from the dialectic:

> Dialectic and dialogic procedures offer two ways of practising a conversation, the one by a play of contraries leading to an agreement, the other by bouncing of views and experiences in an open-ended way.'[19]

In *Together*, Sennett also extensively cites the sixteenth-century *The Book of the Courtier* (1528), by Baldassare Castiglione, which is an early treatise on courtesy and diplomacy. Sidi Larbi Cherkaoui endorses Sennett's valorization of diplomacy as a valuable attitude within a dialogical practice.

> I find diplomacy one of the most important talents that I see around me and that I want to promote. People who are diplomatic question their own desires and are also prepared to let things go.[20]

Sennett is especially touched by the concept of *'sprezzatura,'* an old Italian word that means 'springy' and which Castiglione uses to indicate the importance of keeping diplomatic talk 'light' and 'effortless' allowing for informal, open conversations.[21] Sennett, who himself also had a career as a professional musician, sees the professional performing arts as a particularly well-suited laboratory for retraining our dialogical skills, especially the listening skills which are absolutely necessary 'to become a more cooperative being.' In a good conversation, neither of the participants knows in advance what the topics discussed will be or how the flow and structure of the conversation will connect and link these topics. It is only in the alternation of listening and speaking, of questions and answers, that an associative chain is established. The utterances of everybody participating are usually based on what people already know: their experiences and assumptions. But it is in the shifts of the conversation and in the spaces between utterances that hopefully new insights arise that don't belong to one person specifically, but create a new, shared collective consciousness.

It is because of this intrinsic open quality of the conversation or dialogue that the scientist David Bohm proposes to practice dialogue in larger groups of people to recover a sense of what is 'common' and recreate coherence where there is now mainly fragmentation. Cooperation requires listening and only by doing so are we able to reconcile the complexities of our society, of life in the city, of a group gathering, or a choreography. In *On Dialogue* (1996), Bohm analyses how social coherence in contemporary society is poor because there is a lack of 'shared meaning.'[22] This lack of shared meaning is the result of meaning being fixed in individually held positions. What we need to do, according to Bohm, is to restore 'the flow of meaning' by allowing different voices to coexist. For this we have to practice dialogue. Bohm underlines the importance of listening skills for successful dialogue and acknowledges that new meaning can also arise out of misperception, as well as the inevitable gaps in the flow.

In *Making: Anthropology, Archeology, Art and Architecture* (2013), Tim Ingold offers a valuable semantic alternative to the term 'dialogue' by introducing the notion of 'correspondence,' which can take place not only between humans but also between humans and their animate or inanimate environment, as well as between the craftsman/artist and his materials. Ingold borrows the term 'correspondence' from the increasingly obsolete art of letter writing. He defines two fundamental qualities. Firstly, it is always 'a movement in real time,' which takes time and which 'may go back and forth, without a clear starting point or end point.' Secondly, this 'movement is sentient.'

> On the second point: the lines of correspondence are lines of feeling, of sentience, evinced not—or not only—in the choice of words but in the manual gestures of the writing and their traces on the page. To read a letter is not just to read about one's respondent, but to read with him or her. It is as though the writer was speaking from the page, and you—the reader were there, listening.[23]

Finally, in his book *Conversation Pieces: Community and Communication in Modern Art* (2004), the art historian and critic Grant H. Kester introduces the term 'dialogical art practices' for contemporary art practices that 'share a concern with the creative facilitation of dialogue and exchange,' where 'the conversation is an integral part of the work.'[24] As such, a dialogical art practice always 'unfolds through a process of performative interaction'[25] and shifts its focus from the productive to the receptive side of the creative cycle. 'The artists [...] begin their work not with the desire to express or articulate an already formed creative vision but rather, as [Gemma Corradi Fiumara] has suggested, to listen. Their sense of artistic identity is sufficiently coherent to speak as well as listen, but it remains contingent upon the insights to be derived from their interaction with others and with otherness.'[26]

The work of Sidi Larbi Cherkaoui and Akram Khan doesn't necessarily fit the narrow definition of Kester's 'dialogical art practices' which always involve an active dialogue between artist and audience, but it does incorporate a fundamental dialogical practice with others and with otherness inside its creation process. For me as a dramaturge accompanying them, the dialogical practice is one of the three basic functions and attitudes of my work, alongside that of the witness and of the editor.

Dance Dramaturgy as a Dialogical Practice

> Early, before rehearsals, the most important work happens: conversations that clarify the questions and curiosities that lead to making a piece. We talk about how to work, how to create vocabulary, structure, and meaning. We talk about where to work since different rehearsal spaces produce different shows. We talk about when to work since different schedules produce different shows. We talk about what to do in the rehearsal—what kind of training, how much talking, how much doing: should there be field trips, improvisation?[27]

Maaike Bleeker sees in the dialogue the moment where the dramaturgical reflection of which the choreographer is also capable himself becomes exteriorized in another person, the dramaturge.[28] Dramaturge André Lepecki in his collaboration with Meg Stuart defines the dialogical practice as an 'act of translation' from 'Meg to the dancers, from the dancers to the dancers, from Meg to Meg, from the dancers to Meg, from myself to Meg, from myself to the dancers, and form all of these to all the other collaborators.[29] In his enumeration of dramaturgical activities it is just one of many. For Meg Stuart herself, however, it is the essence of their collaboration: 'A dramaturgical process begins with a dialogue with someone you trust. [...] They are also a big ear with whom I share my initial questions and later my doubts, so as not to spill them all over the studio.'[30] The latter resonates with how Ruth Little describes Akram Khan's desire to work with her. 'At the beginning of our relationship, the choreographers I have worked with expressed to me their desire for an evolving exchange, and they were looking for a dialogue that is testing, supportive, challenging and sensitive to both process and to the nature of the work.'[31]

Other artists such as the Dutch theatre director Jan Joris Lamers define dramaturgy as the 'continuing dialogue'[32] between all the participants of the creative process, regardless of whether there is a dramaturge present or not. In a similar way William Forsythe and his dramaturge Freya Vass-Rhee, at the last *Tanzkongress* in Düsseldorf (2013), describe their collaboration as embedded in a larger dialogue in which all the company members participate. In contrast to some of my colleagues, I define my role as dialogue partner primarily in relationship to the choreographer. I am there first and foremost for him or her and I generally only engage with the other collaborators to moderate between them and the choreographer, when invited to do so. The latter is also a strategy to avoid my voice getting too dominant, or the productive polyphonic conversation becoming a cacophony.

Similarly to how Jacob Zimmer describes the importance of conversation before the start of the rehearsal process, my work as a dramaturge happens as much outside of the studio as inside. Whereas inside the studio the witness role is the more dominant one, outside of it I meet with the choreographer on a regular basis (anywhere from daily to weekly depending on the needs of the process) to discuss what is happening in the studio. These conversations ideally start as early as possible, when the first ideas for a new creation germinate (sometimes while still working on the previous piece) and they intensify during the course of the rehearsal process. These discussions don't so much focus on the material that is developed but on what is needed to further nurture the process: for instance in the communication with the performers, what kind of input they need, how best to plan and organize the time of the rehearsals, how to start thinking about a possible way to organize the material parallel to its development. The time and the place of these conversations is crucial and changes with each choreographer and/or production. Their form, too, requires some reflection. A number of times, for instance, it has taken the form of writing letters—an actual 'correspondence.' In these conversations the act of listening is as important as that of talking. These conversations are also very different from so-called feedback. They are much more open-ended and purposeless. The only kinds of feedback that seem relevant and useful are reminders of previous ideas and conversations, which serve to reconnect with the journey one set out on together. I am a big believer in the notion that in the creative process the first ideas are always the right ones. As such the feedback is often only there to remind the choreographer of these initial, most vital lifelines of the work.

In the case of *zero degrees* (2005), I get involved as a dramaturge relatively late, but I already have a personal relationship with both artists, having presented and co-produced their work at the Arts Centre Vooruit in Ghent. I have also accidentally witnessed several crucial moments in the three-year-long incubation process of getting to know each other and further defining and clarifying their desire to co-create. When they ask me, it is clear that they want and need me most as a moderator. The main part of my work is to listen to both individually expressing their concerns about the process and each other's expectations and anxieties toward it, and to moderate the discussions between them and also with the other artistic collaborators. A good moderator keeps his own voice and opinion out of the discussion. But you do support and reinforce the voice in the discussion that you feel is most relevant in contributing to a solution in which everyone can eventually recognize themselves.

The practical working conditions also define how the different dialogues and conversations take place. Akram still smokes and needs to go out into the street for regular cigarette breaks. I accompany him and use these short breaks to discuss his concerns one-on-one. With Larbi, I am sharing the same guest apartment in London so most of our conversations take place in the evening after rehearsals. For instance, I remember asking him on one of the first nights after rehearsal: 'We know Akram's story, but what is yours?' I don't accept his first evasive answer: 'I tell my story through the stories of others,' and keep insisting. And eventually this leads to him confessing that the story he wants to tell himself is singing *Jerusalem the Golden* which later becomes so significant for the lamentation with which *zero degrees* finishes. If you have a voice as a dramaturge, it is in the way you question things and help the artists to find their own answers.

Similar to Sennett's and Castiglione's concept of *sprezzatura*, I prefer to keep a 'light touch' in my conversations with the artists I accompany. It is a diplomatic art to be able to drop relevant information without too much emphasis on it, so that the dialogue partner, the artist can use it or act upon it at his own discretion and doesn't feel as though being spoken to in an authoritative voice.

A dialogical practice and attitude is fundamental to any creative process in which you want to meet and exchange with the other. It doesn't exclude misunderstandings or disagreements, but it is the only way to interweave different voices polyphonically. If Sidi Larbi Cherkaoui and Akram Khan have been so successful in their relatively short careers, it is mainly because next to their artistic skills, they are also masters of dialogue.

Notes

1   Chambers 1994, p. 31.
2   Fiumara 1990, p. 57.
3   Zappen 2004, p. 3.
4   Ibid., p. 2.
5   Ibid., p. 10.
6   Ibid., pp. 42–43.
7   Abram 1996, p. 113.
8   Ibid., p. 176.
9   Ibid., p. 196.
10 Ibid., p. 244.
11 Corradi Fiumara 1990, p. 8.
12 Ibid., p. 1.
13 Ibid., p. 47.
14 Ibid., p. 108.
15 Ibid., p. 28.
16 Ibid., pp. 166–167.
17 Sennett 2012, pp. 8–9.
18 Ibid., pp. 162–163.
19 Ibid., p. 24.
20 Cherkaoui 2014, p. 253.
21 Sennett, pp. 117–118.
22 Bohm 1996, p. 32.
23 Ingold 2013, p. 105.
24 Kester 2004, p. 8.
25 Ibid., p. 10.
26 Ibid., p. 118.
27 Zimmer 2009, p. 17.
28 Bleeker 2003, p. 166.
29 Lepecki 2010, p. 66.
30 Stuart 2010, p. 134.
31 Ruth Little in Trencsényi 2015, p. 223.
32 Lamers 1994, pp. 286–287.

Bibliography

– Abram, David. *The Spell of the Sensuous.* New York: Random House, 1996.

– Albright, Ann Cooper. 'Moving Contexts.' In *Dance: Distinct Language and Cross-Cultural Influences,* edited by Chantal Pontbriand, pp. 41–51. Montréal: Parachute, 2001.

– Albright, Ann Cooper. *Choreographing Difference: The Body and Identity in Contemporary Dance.* Middletown: Wesleyan University Press, 1997.

– Anderson, Zoe. Review of *Desh* by Akram Khan. *The Independent,* 10 October 2011.

– Assmann, Jan. 'Re-Membering Osiris: From the Death Cult to Cultural Memory.' In *ReMembering the Body,* edited by Gabriele Brandstetter and Hortensia Volckers, pp. 42–78. Ostfildern: Hatje Cantz, 2000.

– Banes, Sally. 'Our Hybrid Tradition.' In *Dance Distinct Language and Cross-Cultural influences,* edited by Chantal Pontbriand, pp. 21–30. Montréal: Parachute, 2001.

– Bauman, Zygmunt. 'From Pilgrim to Tourist—or a Short History of Identity.' In *Questions of Cultural Identity,* edited by Stuart Hall and Paul du Gay, pp. 18–36. London: Sage Publications, 1996.

– Benjamin, Walter. 'The Task of the Translator: An Introduction to the Translation of Baudelaire's *Tableaux Parisiens*' [1923]. Translated by Harry Zohn. In *The Translation Studies Reader,* edited by Lawrence Venuti, pp. 15–25. New York: Routledge, 2000.

– Berger, John. *Hold Everything Dear: Dispatches on Survival and Resistance.* London: Verso, 2007.

– Bhabha, Homi K. *Uber Kulturelle Hybridität.* Translated by Kathrina Menke. Vienna: Turia + Kant, 2012.

– Bhabha, Homi K. *The Location of Culture.* New York: Routledge, 1994.

– Bhabha, Homi K. 'Culture's In-Between.' In *Questions of Cultural Identity,* edited by Stuart Hall and Paul du Gay, pp. 53–60. London: Sage Publications, 1996.

– Bleeker, Maaike. 'Dramaturgy as a Mode of Looking.' *Women & Performance: a Journal of Feminist Theory* 13, no. 2 (2003), pp. 163–172.

– Bogart, Anne. *What's the Story: Essays about Art, Theater and Storytelling.* London: Routledge, 2014.

– Bohm, David. *On Dialogue.* London: Routledge, 1996.

– Boisseau, Rosita. *Sidi Larbi Cherkaoui.* Paris: Éditions Textuel, 2013.

– Braidotti, Rosi. 'Nomadic European Identity.' In *No Culture, No Europe: On the Foundation of Politics,* edited by Pascal Gielen, pp. 97–113. Amsterdam: Valiz, 2015.

– Braidotti, Rosi. *Nomadic Theory: The Portable Rosi Braidotti.* New York: Columbia University Press, 2011.

– Brown, Ismene. 'Marvellous Hybrid Kicks Like a Mule.' Review of Akram Khan at Sadler's Wells. *Daily Telegraph,* 14 July 2005.

– Buckmaster, Sue. *A Psychoanalytical Study of the Power of the Puppet.* MA thesis (unpublished), University of Essex, Colchester, UK, 1997.

– Burt, Ramsay. 'Resistant Identities: Anderson and Ruckert.' In *Dance Discourses: Keywords in Dance Research,* edited by Susanne Franco and Marina Nordera, pp. 208–209. London: Routledge, 2007.

– Burt, Ramsay. 'Contemporary Dance and the Performance of Multicultural Identities.' Paper presented at Conference on Research in Dance, Ministry of Culture Committee on Sports Research, Copenhagen, 8–9 January 2004. www.akramkhancompany.net/html/akram_essay.php?id=15. Accessed May 2015.

– Chambers, Iain. *Migrancy, Culture, Identity.* London: Routledge, 1994.

– Chatterjea, Ananya. 'Red-stained Feet: Probing the Ground on Which Women Dance in Contemporary Bengal.' In *Worlding Dance,* edited by Susan Leigh Foster, pp. 119–143. Studies in International Performance, edited by Janelle Reinelt and Brian Singleton. London: Palgrave Macmillan, 2009.

– Cherkaoui, Sidi Larbi, and Lise Uytterhoeven. 'On Collaboration and Navigating between Dance Cultures: an Ethics of Reconciliation.' In *The Ethics of Art: Ecological Turns in the Performing Arts,* edited by Guy Cools and Pascal Gielen, pp. 247–258. Amsterdam: Valiz, 2014.

– Cherkaoui, Sidi Larbi. 'De undercover-Arabier.' *MO*, 4 March 2014. www.mo.be/column/de-undercover-arabier. Accessed May 2015.

– Cherkaoui, Sidi Larbi. 'Eén achter-naam, veel toekomst.' *MO*, 28 January 2014. www.mo.be/artikel/een-achter-naam-veel-toekomst. Accessed May 2015.

- Cherkaoui, Sidi Larbi. 'State of the Union.' Talk, *Theaterfestival*, Tilburg, NL, 22 August 2008. www.dansendansen.be/ekfinder/userfiles/files/state-of-the-union-08–Sidi-Larbi-Cherkaoui.pdf. Accessed May 2015.
- Cherkaoui, Sidi Larbi and Gilles Delmas (with Karthika Nair and Jules Morin). *Zon-Mai, Parcours Nomades.* Arles: Actes Sud/Cité nationale de l'histoire de l'immigration, 2007.
- Cherkaoui, Sidi Larbi. 'Eer en schuld.' In *Toneelg(e)ruis* 1, pp. 71–81. Antwerp: Toneelhuis, 2006a.
- Cherkaoui, Sidi Larbi, and Justin Morin. *Pèlerinage sur soi.* Arles: Actes Sud, 2006b.
- Cherkaoui, Sidi Larbi. 'Een roller-coaster van emoties.' In *Toneelg(e)ruis* 0, pp. 47–53. Antwerp: Toneelhuis, 2006c.
- *Akram Khan: Homeland, The Making of Desh.* DVD. Directed by Joanne Coates. London: Moonspun Films, 2011.
- Bal, Mieke. 'Lost in Space, Lost in the Library.' In *Essays in Migratory Aesthetics: Cultural Practices Between Migration and Art-making,* edited by Sam Durrant and Catherine M. Lord, pp. 23–35. Thamyris/Intersecting: Place, Sex, and Race 17, edited by Ernst van Alphen. Amsterdam: Rodopi, 2007.
- Cools, Guy. 'Re-membering Zero Degrees.' In *New Dramaturgy: International Perspectives,* edited by Bernadette Cochrane and Katalin Trencsényi, pp. 180–194. London: Metheun, 2014a.
- Cools, Guy. 'The Art of Listening.' In *The Ethics of Art: Ecological Turns in the Performing Arts,* edited by Guy Cools and Pascal Gielen, pp. 43–55. Amsterdam: Valiz, 2014b.
- Cools, Guy. 'Soms is het prettig om op je hoofd te staan en zo de wereld te bekijken.' *Etcetera,* no. 137 (2014c), pp. 3–9.
- Cools, Guy. *body:language #1 Sidi Larbi Cherkaoui.* London: Sadler's Wells, 2012a.
- Cools, Guy. *body:language #2 Akram Khan.* London: Sadler's Wells, 2012b.
- Cools, Guy. 'Nomadisme als ankerpunt.' In *Dans in Québec,* edited by Samme Raeymaekers, pp. 11–30. Ghent: Borgerhoff & Lamberigts, 2008.
- Cools, Guy. 'L'Homme kaleidoscope, een gesprek met Sidi Larbi Cherkaoui.' In *Toneelg(e)ruis* 2, pp. 111–121. Antwerp: Toneelhuis, 2007.
- Cools, Guy. 'Polyfoon bewegen: Guy Cools over Sidi Larbi Cherkaoui.' In *Toneelg(e)ruis* 0, pp. 37–45. Antwerp: Toneelhuis, 2006.
- Cools, Guy. *Programme Note, zero degrees.* London: Sadler's Wells, 2005.
- Cools, Guy. 'Dance: A Translating Art: The Body as a "Transmuter" of Identity.' In *Dance: Distinct Language and Cross-Cultural influences,* edited by Chantal Pontbriand, pp. 31–40. Parachute: Montréal, 2001.
- Corradi Fiumara, Gemma. *The Other Side of Language: A Philosophy of Listening.* London: Routledge, 1990.
- *Sidi Larbi Cherkaoui: Alle dansers zijn Migranten.* Goudvis Documentary. DVD. Directed by Guido De Bruyn. Brussels: Canvas, 2011.
- *The Six Seasons.* DVD. Directed by Gilles Delmas. Paris: Lardux Films, 2012.
- *Zero Degrees, Infinity.* DVD. Directed by Gilles Delmas. Paris: Lardux Films, 2006.
- De Riencourt, Amaury. *The Eye of Shiva: Eastern Mysticism and Science.* London: Souvenir Press, 1980.
- De Somviele, Charlotte. 'All Eyes in Dance World on Sidi Larbi Cherkaoui.' *Flanders Today,* 16 February 2015.
- Derrida, Jacques. 'Living On,' translated by James Hulbert. In *Deconstruction and Criticism,* edited by Harold Bloom, pp. 75–176. London: Routledge, 1979.
- Dougil, David. 'Two of a Kind.' Review of *zero degrees* by Sidi Larbi Cherkaoui and Akram Khan. *Sunday Times,* 17 July 2005.
- Durrant, Sam and Catherine M. Lord, eds. *Essays in Migratory Aesthetics: Cultural Practices Between Migration and Art-making.* Thamyris/Intersecting: Place, Sex, and Race 17, edited by Ernst van Alphen. Amsterdam: Rodopi, 2007.
- Enzensberger, Hans Magnus. 'The State of Europe.' *Granta* 30, pp. 136–142. Cambridge, UK: Granta Publications, 1990.
- Fischer-Lichte, Erika, Torsten Jost, and Saskya Iris Jain, eds. *The Politics of Interweaving Performance Cultures: Beyond Postcolonialism.* New York: Routledge, 2014.
- Foster, Susan Leigh. 'Jérôme Bel and Myself: Gender and Intercultural Collaboration.' In *Emerging Bodies: The Performance of Worldmaking in Dance and Choreography,* edited by Gabriele Klein and Sandra Noeth, pp. 73–81. Bielefeld: Transcript, 2011.

Franco, Susanne and Marina Nordera, eds. *Dance Discourses: Keywords in Dance Research.* London: Routledge, 2007.

Frater, Sarah. Review of *Desh* by Akram Khan. *Evening Standard,* 5 October 2011.

Frater, Sarah. 'Opposites Seek a Seminal Moment.' Review of *zero degrees* by Sidi Larbi Cherkaoui and Akram Khan. *Evening Standard,* 13 July 2005.

Ghose, Sumantro. 'A Fusion of Many Worlds.' Review of *zero degrees* by Sidi Larbi Cherkaoui and Akram Khan. *The Independent,* 8 July 2005.

Gielen, Pascal, and Rudi Laermans. 'Constructing Identities: The Case of "the Flemish Dance Wave."' In *Europe Dancing: Perspectives on Theatre Dance and Cultural Identity,* edited by Andrée Grau and Stephanie Jordan, pp. 12–24. London: Routledge, 2000.

Gilbert, Jenny. 'Stop that Train, I Want to Get On.' Review of *zero degrees* by Sidi Larbi Cherkaoui and Akram Khan. *The Independent on Sunday,* 17 July 2005.

Gormley, Antony. *Independent,* 22 April 2004, p. 16.

Grau, Andrée. 'Dance, Identity, and Identification Processes in the Postcolonial World.' In *Dance Discourses: Keywords in Dance Research,* edited by Susanne Franco and Marina Nordera, pp. 189–207. London: Routledge, 2007.

Graham, Martha. *Blood Memory: An Autobiography.* New York: Doubleday, 1991.

Grau, Andrée. 'A Sheltering Sky? Negotiating Identity through South Asian Dance.' In Shiromi Pinto, *No Man's Land: Exploring South Asianness,* 25 June 2004. Report on symposium at Institute for Contemporary Art, London, 22 May 2004. http://akademi.co.uk/wp-content/uploads/2014/02/No-Mans-Land-Report.pdf. Accessed June 2015.

Grau, Andrée, and Stephanie Jordan, eds. *Europe Dancing: Perspectives on Theatre Dance and Cultural Identity.* London: Routledge, 2000.

Gross, Kenneth. *Puppet: An Essay on Uncanny Life.* Chicago: University of Chicago Press, 2011.

Grossberg, Lawrence. 'Identity and Cultural Studies—Is That All There is?,' In *Questions of Cultural Identity,* edited by Stuart Hall and Paul du Gay, pp. 87–107. London: Sage Publications, 1996.

Hall, Stuart, and Paul du Gay, eds. *Questions of Cultural Identity.* London: Sage Publications, 1996.

Hall, Stuart. 'Who needs "Identity?,"' In *Questions of Cultural Identity,* edited by Stuart Hall and Paul du Gay, pp. 1–17. London: Sage Publications, 1996.

Hallam, Elizabeth, and Tim Ingold, eds. *Creativity and Cultural Improvisation.* Oxford: Berg, 2007.

Hatrak, Ketu H. *Contemporary Indian Dance: New Creative Choreography in India and the Diaspora.* New York: Palgrave MacMillan, 2011.

Huggan, Graham. 'Unsettled Settlers: Postcolonialism, Travelling Theory and the New Migrant Aesthetics.' In *Essays in Migratory Aesthetics: Cultural Practices Between Migration and Art-making,* edited by Sam Durrant and Catherine M. Lord, pp. 129–143. Thamyris/Intersecting: Place, Sex, and Race 17, edited by Ernst van Alphen. Amsterdam: Rodopi, 2007.

Hutera, Donald. Review of *Desh* by Akram Khan. *Dance Magazine,* 5 October 2011.

Ingold, Tim. *Making: Anthropology, Archaeology, Art and Architecture.* London: Routledge, 2013.

Ingold, Tim. *Being Alive: Essays on Movement, Knowledge and Description.* London: Routledge, 2011.

Ishiguro, Kazuo. *An Artist of the Floating World.* London: Faber and Faber, 1986.

Jans, Erwin. 'Het culturele verschil ligt soms ver van mijn bed: Een gesprek met Sidi Larbi Cherkaoui.' In *Toneelg(e)ruis* 4, pp. 115–121. Antwerp: Toneelhuis, 2009.

Jans, Erwin. 'Let's Crash, not Clash.' In *Toneelg(e)ruis* 1, pp. 139–142. Antwerp: Toneelhuis, 2006.

Jennings, Luke. Review of *Desh* by Akram Khan. *The Guardian,* 17 September 2011.

Jodorowsky, Alexander. *La Voie du Tarot.* Paris: Éditions Albin, 2004.

Jordan, Stephanie. 'Cultural Crossings: Containing the Crisis...and the Indian in our Midst.' In *Dance: Distinct Language and Cross-Cultural Influences,* edited by Chantal Pontbriand, pp. 111–120. Montréal: Parachute, 2001.

Keleman, Stanley. *Myth & the Body: A Colloquy with Joseph Campbell.* Berkeley: Center Press, 1999.

Dreams of Babel. DVD. Directed by Don Kent. Paris: ARTE and Bel Air Media, 2009.

- Kérouanton, Joël. 'Over Myth.' In *Toneelg(e)ruis 2*, pp. 175-191. Antwerp: Toneelhuis, 2007.
- Kérouanton, Joël. *Sidi Larbi Cherkaoui, Rencontres*. Paris: L'œil d'or, 2004.
- Kester, Grant H. *Conversation Pieces: Community and Communication in Modern Art*. Los Angeles: University of California Press, 2004.
- Khumalo, George Mxolisi. 'Processen die tijd nodig hebben: In gesprek met Marianne Van Kerkhoven.' *Etcetera* 87 (2003), pp. 7-10.
- Klein, Gabriele, and Sandra Noeth, eds. *Emerging Bodies: The Performance of Worldmaking in Dance and Choreography*. Bielefeld: Transcript, 2011.
- Kristeva, Julia. *Strangers to Ourselves*. New York: Harvester Wheatsheaf, 1991.
- Lambrechts, An-Marie. 'Absolute empathie, Interview met Sidi Larbi Cherkaoui.' In *Toneelg(e)ruis 5*. pp. 35-41. Antwerp: Toneelhuis, 2010.
- Lamers, Jan Joris. 'A Continuing Dialogue, in: Van Kerkhoven.' In 'On Dramaturgy,' edited by Marianne Van Kerkhoven et al. Special issue. *Theaterschrift* 5-6 (1994), pp. 278-303.
- Lepecki, André. 'Dramaturging: A Quasi-objective Gaze on Anti-memory.' In *Are We Here Yet?*, edited by Jeroen Peeters, pp. 64-71. Dijon: presses du réel, 2010.
- Lepecki, André. 'For a Sensorial Manifesto (On Dances that Failed).' In *Dance: Distinct Language and Cross-Cultural Influences*, edited by Chantal Pontbriand, pp. 161-168. Montréal: Parachute, 2001.
- Levy, Liesbeth. 'The dilemma of the double double bind.' In *Common Skin*, edited by Daphne Pappers, pp. 73-89. Context Without Walls, edited by Daphne Pappers. Amsterdam: Valiz, 2014.
- Lopez y Royo, Alessandra. 'Classicism, Post-Classicism, and Ranjabati Sircar's Work.' *South Asia Research* 23, no. 2 (November 2003), pp. 153-169.
- Mackrell, Judith. Review of *Babel* by Sidi Larbi Cherkaoui. *The Guardian*, 19 May 2010.
- Mackrell, Judith. Review of *Opposites Attract* performed by the Royal Ballet. *The Guardian*, 12 July 2005.
- Malouf, Amin. *Identités Meurtrières*. Paris: Grasset, 1998.
- Meduri, Avanthi. 'Geo-politics, Dissensus, and Dance Citizenship: the Case of South Asian Dance in Britain.' In *Dance [and] Theory*, edited by Gabriele Brandstetter and Gabriele Klein, pp. 177-182. Bielefeld: Transcript, 2013.
- Mitra, Royona. *Akram Khan: Dancing New Interculturalism*. Basingstoke: Palgrave MacMillan, 2015.
- Mitra, Royona. 'Dancing Embodiment, Theorizing Space: Exploring the "Third Space" in Akram Khan's zero degrees.' In *Planes of Composition: Dance, Theory and the Global*, edited by Joy Jenn and André Lepecki, pp. 40-63. New York: Seagull Press, 2009.
- Monahan, Mark. Review of *Desh* by Akram Khan. *Telegraph*, 5 October 2011.
- Nair, Karthika. *Desh, Un Voyage de création*. Grenoble: MC2, 2010.
- Nair, Karthika. *bearings*. Noida, IND: HarperCollins, 2009.
- Nair, Karthika. 'Gezocht: zelf.' In *Toneelg(e)ruis 3*, pp. 106-117. Antwerp: Toneelhuis, 2008.
- Navtej, Johar. 'The Power of Seeing: Body, History and the City.' In *The Ethics of Art: Ecological Turns in the Performing Arts*, edited by Guy Cools and Pascal Gielen, pp. 299-317. Amsterdam: Valiz, 2014.
- Norman, Neil. Review of Desh by Akram Khan. *Daily Express*, 7 October 2011.
- Pontbriand, Chantal, ed. *Dance: Distinct Language and Cross-Cultural Influences*. Montréal: Parachute, 2001.
- Ramachandran, Vilayanur. 'The Neurons that Shaped Civilization.' Talk, TEDIndia, conference, Mysore, India, 4-6 November 2009. www.ted.com/talks/vs_ramchandran_ the_neurons_that_shaped_ civilization.html. Accessed May 2015.
- Robins, Kevin. 'Interrupting Identities: Turkey/Europe.' In *Questions of Cultural Identity*, edited by Stuart Hall and Paul du Gay, pp. 61-86. London: Sage Publications, 1996.
- Rushdie, Salman. 'Step Across This Line: The Tanner Lectures on Human Values.' In *Step Across This Line: Collected Non-Fiction: 1992-2002*, pp. 405-442. London: Vintage, 2003.
- Rushdie, Salman. *The Satanic Verses*. London: Penguin, 1988.
- Sanders, Lorna. '"I just Can't Wait to Get to the Hotel": *zero degrees*.' Essay, 2005. www.akramkhancom-pany.net/ckfinderuserfiles/files/ AKCT%20zerodegrees-1%20by%20 Lorna.pdf. Accessed May 2015.

Sanders, Lorna. *Akram Khan's Rush: Creative Insights*. Alton, UK: Dance Books, 2004.

Scarry, Elaine. *On Beauty and Being Just*. Princeton: Princeton University Press, 1999.

Schirren, Fernand. *Le rythme primordial et souverain*. Brussels: Contredanse, 1996.

Sennett, Richard. *Together, the Rituals, Pleasures and Politics of Cooperation*. London: Allan Lane, 2012.

Sennett, Richard. *The Foreigner: Two Essays on Exile*. London: Notting Hill Editions, 2011.

Shah, Asma. 'Working Internationally: An Interview with Farooq Chaudhry.' London, September 2010. www.akramkhancompany.net/ckfinder/userfiles/files/Working%20Internationally%20-%20An%20with%20Farooq%20Chaudhry.pdf. Accessed May 2015.

Sibony, Daniel. *Le corps et sa danse*. Paris: Éditions du Seuil, 1995.

Sibony, Daniel. *Entre-deux: L'origine en partage*. Paris: Éditions du Seuil, 1991.

Solnit, Rebecca. *A Paradise Built in Hell*. New York: Penguin, 2009.

Strathern, Marilyn. 'Enabling Identity? Biology, Choice and New Reproductive Technologies.' In *Questions of Cultural Identity*, edited by Stuart Hall and Paul du Gay, pp. 37-52. London: Sage Publications, 1996.

Stuart, Meg. 'The Big Ear.' In *Are We Here Yet?*, edited by Jeroen Peeters, pp. 134-135. Dijon: presses du réel, 2010.

Sulcas, Roslyn. 'Silk Monsoons Cascade into a Homeland Tale.' Review of *Desh* by Akram Khan. *New York Times*, 7 October 2011.

Surowiecki, James. *The Wisdoms of the Crowds: Why the Many Are Smarter than the Few and How Collective Wisdom Shapes Business, Economies, Societies and Nations*. New York: Doubleday, 2004.

Thich Nhat Hanh. *Bouddha et Jésus sont des frères*. Gordes: Éditions du Relié, 2001.

Trencsényi, Katalin. *Dramaturgy in the Making: A User's Guide for Theatre Practitioners*. London: Bloomsbury, 2015.

Uytterhoeven, Lise. *New Dramaturgies in the Work of Sidi Larbi Cherkaoui*. PhD dissertation (unpublished), University of Surrey, Guildford, UK, 2013.

Uytterhoeven, Lise. 'Dreams, Myth, History: Sidi Larbi Cherkaoui's Dramaturgies.' *Contemporary Theatre Review* 21, no. 3 (2011), pp. 332-339.

Wiegand, Chris. *Akram Khan Portrait Unveiled*. Review of Akram Khan portrait by Darvish Fakhr. *The Guardian*, 1 October 2008.

Zappen, James P. *The Rebirth of Dialogue: Bakhtin, Socrates, and the Rhetorical Tradition*. New York: State University of New York Press, 2004.

Zimmer, Jacob. 'Friendship is No Day Job and Other Thoughts of a Resident Dance Dramaturg.' In *Canadian Theatre Review* 155 (Summer 2003). Dance and Movement Dramaturgy, edited by Pil Hansen, Darcey Callison, and Bruce Barton, pp. 16-20. Toronto: University of Toronto Press, 2003.

Zukav, Gary. *The Dancing Wuli Masters*. London: Random House, 1979.

Bibliography

133

About the Author

Guy Cools is a dance dramaturge. Recent positions include Associate Professor for Dance Studies at the research institute Arts in Society of the Fontys School of Fine and Performing Arts in Tilburg (NL), and at Ghent University (BE), where he finished a practice-based PhD on the relationship between dance and writing. He has worked as a dance critic, artistic programmer, and policymaker for dance in Flanders. He now dedicates himself to production dramaturgy, contributing to work by choreographers all over Europe and Canada such as: Koen Augustijnen (BE), Sidi Larbi Cherkaoui (BE), Danièle Desnoyers (CA), Lia Haraki (CY), Christopher House (CA), Akram Khan (UK), Arno Schuitemaker (NL), and Stephanie Thiersch (DE). He regularly lectures and publishes, and has developed a series of workshops that aim to support artists and choreographers in their creative process. His most recent publications include *The Ethics of Art: Ecological Turns in the Performing Arts*, co-edited with Pascal Gielen (Valiz, 2014) and the series *Body:Language* (Sadler's Wells, 2008–2011). With the Canadian choreographer, Lin Snelling, he developed an improvised performance practice 'Rewriting Distance' that focuses on the integration of movement, voice, and writing. See also: www.rewritingdistance.com.

Arts in Society Series

In-between Dance Cultures: The Migratory Artistic Identity of Sidi Larbi Cherkaoui and Akram Khan is the 21st publication in a series of books that map the interaction between changes in society and cultural practices. Inspired by art and critical theory, the series *Arts* in *Society* studies the possibilities of a repositioning of the arts and culture in society. The series is open for publishing proposals in the form of essays, theoretical explanations, practice-oriented research in the arts, and research studies.

Editor-in-chief
Pascal Gielen
p.j.d.gielen@rug.nl

Index

A

A Filetta 64
Abram, David 115, 116
Academy of Indian Dance 69
Acquaviva, Jean-Claude 64
Adichie, Chimamanda Ngozi 36
Agudo, Jose 104
AKCT (Advanced Kathak and Choreographic Training) 71
Akram Khan Company, London 9, 51, 72, 74, 93
Albright, Ann Cooper 52, 53
Anna Karenina 67
Anonymous Society 62
Apocrifu 19, 64, 91, 92
Arts Centre Vooruit, Ghent 15, 18, 24, 57, 73, 110, 122
Assmann, Jan 45
Association of European Cities and Region for Culture 28

B

Babel[(words)] 65–67, 98, 99, 102, 106, 107, 111
Bahok 19, 41, 68, 73-75, 94–96, 111
Bakhtin, Mikhail 31, 114, 115, 118
Bal, Mieke 20
Balanchine, George 51
Ballets C de la B, Les, Ghent 9, 62, 63
Ballets de Monte-Carlo, Les 34, 63
Banes, Sally 51–53
Bauman, Zygmunt 30, 37
Bausch, Pina 44, 95
Béjart, Maurice 110
Bel, Jérôme 39
Benjamin, Walter 52
Berger, John 94
Berliner Zeitung 28
Bhabha, Homi K. 22, 29, 31, 32, 35, 36, 56, 94
Binoche, Juliette 74, 81
Bleeker, Maaike 120
Bogart, Anne 46
Bohm, David 119
Boléro 99
Bouche, Iris 86, 92
Bourgeouis, Louise 45

Colophon

Colophon

In-between Dance Cultures
*On the Migratory Artistic Identity
of Sidi Larbi Cherkaoui and
Akram Khan*

Author
Guy Cools

Antennae Series N° 21
by Valiz, Amsterdam

Part of the Series
'Arts *in* Society"

Editing
Lisa Marie Bowler

Copy editing
Janine Armin

Proof Check
Els Brinkman

Index
Elke Stevens

Production
Pia Pol

Design
Metahaven

Paper inside
Munken Print 100 gr 1.5

Paper cover
Bioset 240 gr

Printing and binding
Ten Brink, Meppel

Publisher
Valiz, Amsterdam, 2015
www.valiz.nl

We have kindly received permission
to reproduce Karhtika Nair's
poem 'zero degrees: between
boundaries' on page 82, originally
published in *bearings*, Noida, IND:
HarperCollins, 2009.

ISBN 978-94-92095-11-4

This publication was made possible
through the generous support of

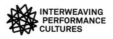

Interweaving Performance Cultures,
of the Freie Universität Berlin

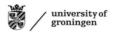

University of Groningen
www.rug.nl

The authors and the publisher have made every effort to secure permission to reproduce the listed material, illustrations and photographs. We apologise for any inadvert errors or omissions. Parties who nevertheless believe they can claim specific legal rights are invited to contact the publisher.

Distribution:
USA /Canada/Latin America: D.A.P., www.artbook.com
GB/IE: Anagram Books, www.anagrambooks.com
NL/BE/LU: Coen Sligting, www.coensligtingbookimport.nl
Europe/Asia/Australia: Idea Books, www.ideabooks.nl

ISBN 978-94-92095-11-4
NUR 675

Printed and bound in the Netherlands

Antennae

Antennae Series

Antennae N° 1
The Fall of the Studio
Artists at Work
edited by Wouter Davidts
& Kim Paice
Amsterdam: Valiz, 2009
(2nd ed.: 2010),
ISBN 978-90-78088-29-5

Antennae N° 2
Take Place
*Photography and Place
from Multiple Perspectives*
edited by Helen Westgeest
Amsterdam: Valiz, 2009,
ISBN 978-90-78088-35-6

Antennae N° 3
**The Murmuring of the
Artistic Multitude**
Global Art, Memory and Post-Fordism
Pascal Gielen (author)
Arts *in* Society
Amsterdam: Valiz, 2009
(2nd ed.: 2011),
ISBN 978-90-78088-34-9

Antennae N° 4
Locating the Producers
Durational Approaches to Public Art
edited by Paul O'Neill
& Claire Doherty
Amsterdam: Valiz, 2011,
ISBN 978-90-78088-51-6

Antennae N° 5
Community Art
The Politics of Trespassing
edited by Paul De Bruyne &
Pascal Gielen
Arts *in* Society
Amsterdam: Valiz, 2011 (2nd ed.: 2013),
ISBN 978-90-78088-50-9

Antennae N° 6
See it Again, Say it Again
The Artist as Researcher
edited by Janneke Wesseling
Amsterdam: Valiz, 2011,
ISBN 978-90-78088-53-0

Antennae N° 7
**Teaching Art in the
Neoliberal Realm**
Realism versus Cynicism
edited by Pascal Gielen &
Paul De Bruyne
Arts *in* Society
Amsterdam: Valiz, 2012
(2nd ed.: 2013),
ISBN 978-90-78088-57-8

Antennae N° 8
Institutional Attitudes
Instituting Art in a Flat World
edited by Pascal Gielen
Arts *in* Society
Amsterdam: Valiz, 2013,
ISBN 978-90-78088-68-4

Antennae N° 9
Dread
The Dizziness of Freedom
edited by Juha van 't Zelfde
Amsterdam: Valiz, 2013,
ISBN 978-90-78088-81-3

Antennae N° 10
Participation Is Risky
Approaches to Joint Creative Processes
edited by Liesbeth Huybrechts
Amsterdam: Valiz, 2014,
ISBN 978-90-78088-77-6

Antennae N° 11
The Ethics of Art
Ecological Turns in the Performing Arts
edited by Guy Cools & Pascal Gielen
Arts *in* Society
Amsterdam: Valiz, 2014,
ISBN 978-90-78088-87-5

Antennae N° 12
Alternative Mainstream
Making Choices in Pop Music
Gert Keunen (author)
Arts *in* Society
Amsterdam: Valiz, 2014,
ISBN 978-90-78088-95-0

Antennae N° 13
The Murmuring of the Artistic Multitude
Global Art, Politics and Post-Fordism
Pascal Gielen (author)
Completely revised and enlarged
edition of Antennae N° 3
Arts *in* Society
Amsterdam: Valiz, 2015,
ISBN 978-94-92095-04-6

Antennae N° 14
Aesthetic Justice
Intersecting Artistic and Moral Perspectives
edited by Pascal Gielen &
Niels Van Tomme
Arts *in* Society
Amsterdam: Valiz, 2015,
ISBN 978-90-78088-86-8

Antennae N° 15
No Culture, No Europe
On the Foundation of Politics
edited by Pascal Gielen
Arts *in* Society
Amsterdam: Valiz, 2015,
ISBN 978-94-92095-03-9

Antennae N° 16
Arts Education Beyond Art
Teaching Art in Times of Change
edited by Barend van Heusden &
Pascal Gielen
Arts *in* Society
Amsterdam: Valiz, 2015,
ISBN 978-90-78088-85-1

Antennae N° 17
Mobile Autonomy
Exercises in Artists' Self-Organization
edited by Nico Dockx &
Pascal Gielen
Arts *in* Society
Amsterdam: Valiz, 2015,
ISBN 978-94-92095-10-7

Antennae N° 18
Moving Together
*Theorizing and Making
Contemporary Dance*
Rudi Laermans (author)
Arts *in* Society
Amsterdam: Valiz, 2015.
ISBN 978-90-78088-52-3

Antennae N° 19
Spaces for Criticism
Shifts in Contemporary Art Discourses
Thijs Lijster, Suzana Milevska,
Pascal Gielen, Ruth Sonderegger
Arts *in* Society
Amsterdam: Valiz, 2015.
ISBN 978-90-78088-75-2

Antennae N° 20
Interrupting the City
*Artistic Constitutions of the
Public Sphere*
Sander Bax, Pascal Gielen,
Bram Ieven (eds.)
Arts *in* Society
Amsterdam: Valiz, 2015.
ISBN 978-94-92095-02-2

CW00683894

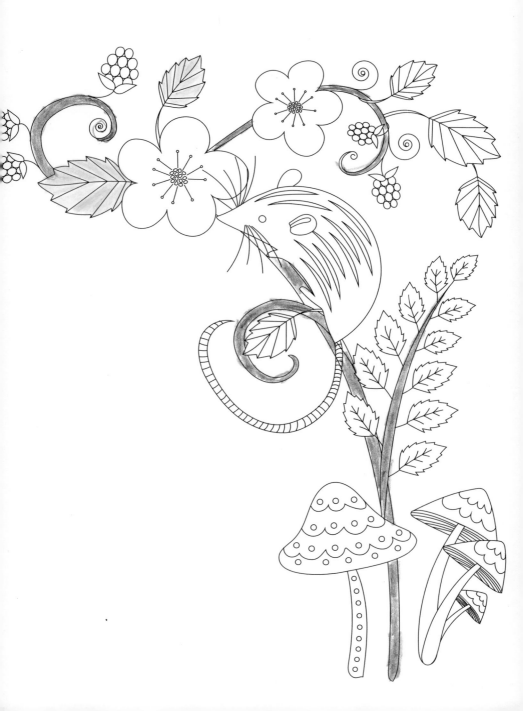

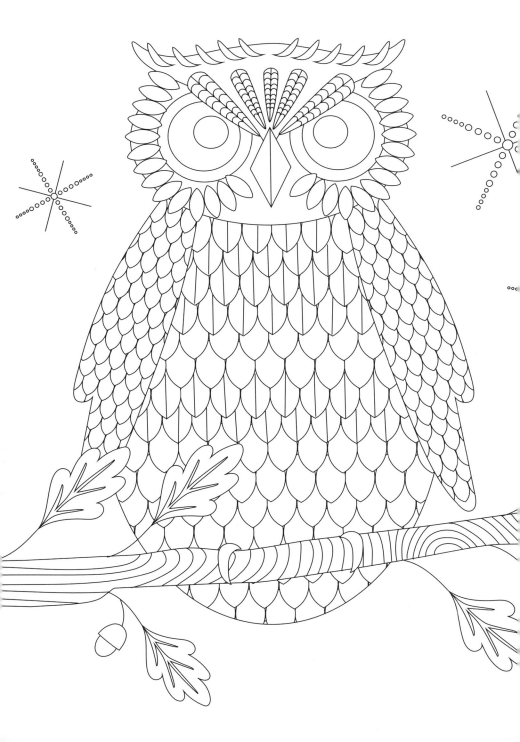

"In today's rush we all think too much,
seek too much, want too much and forget
about the joy of just being."

Eckhart Tolle

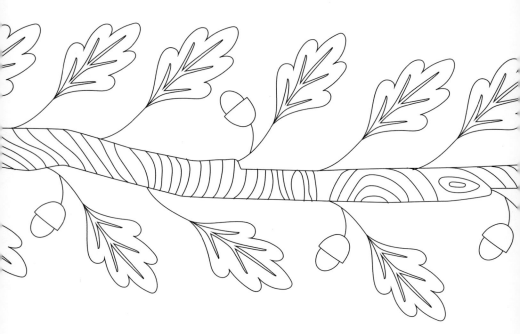

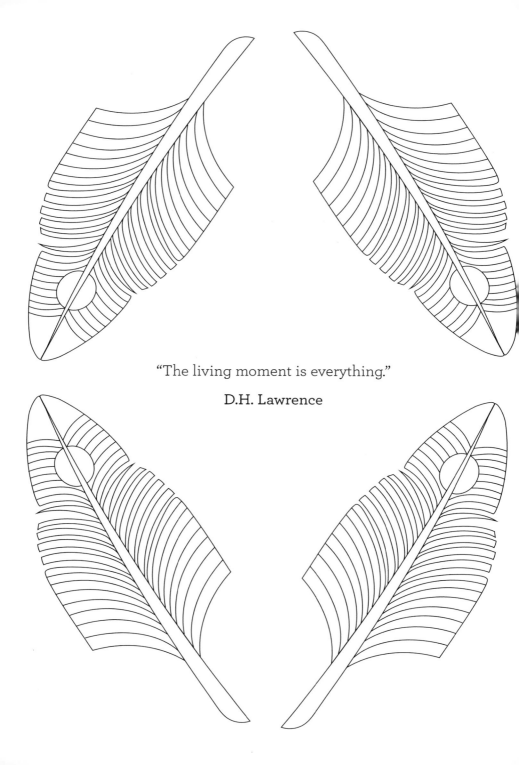

"The living moment is everything."

D.H. Lawrence

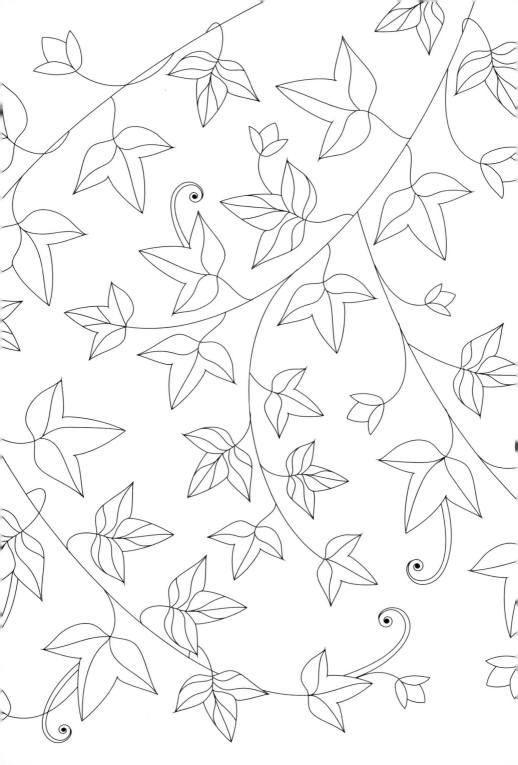

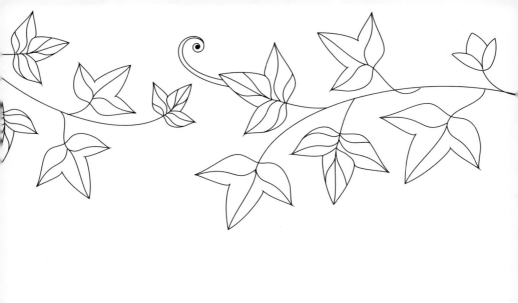

"Look within. Within is the fountain
of good, and it will ever bubble up,
if thou wilt ever dig."

Marcus Aurelius

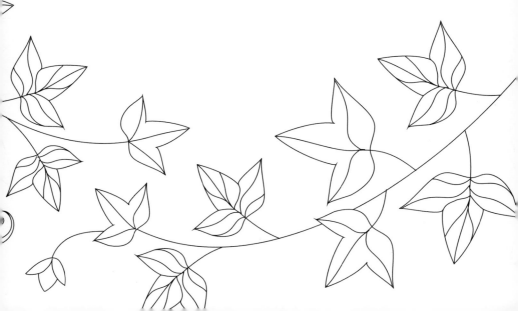

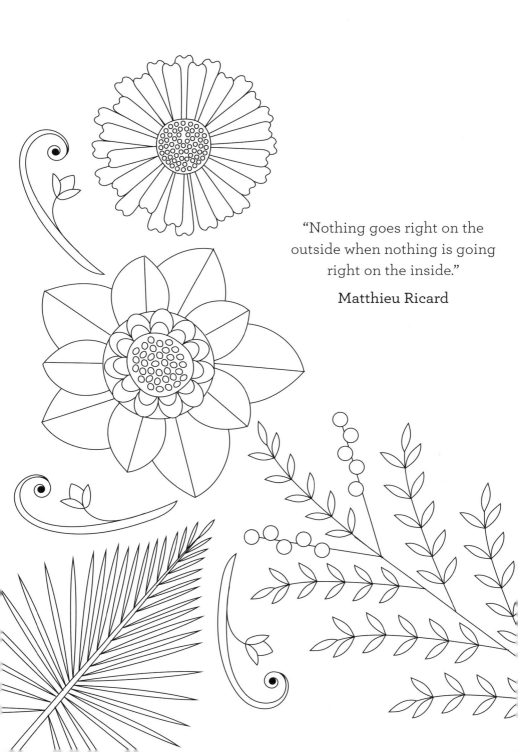

"Nothing goes right on the outside when nothing is going right on the inside."

Matthieu Ricard

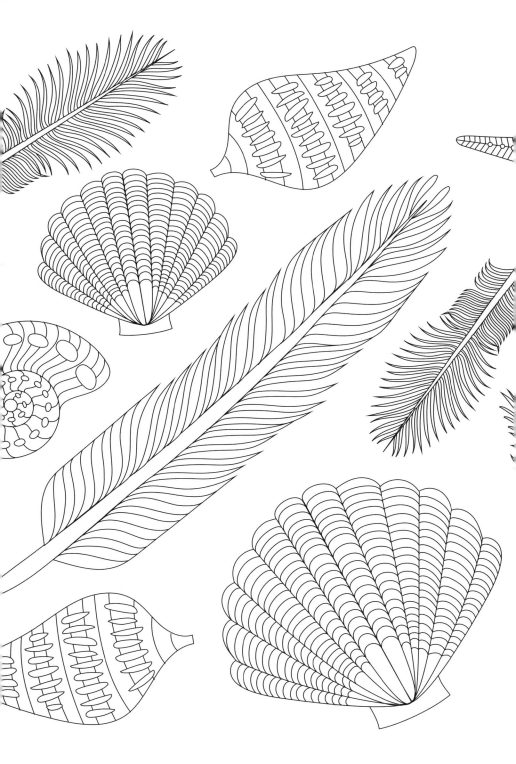

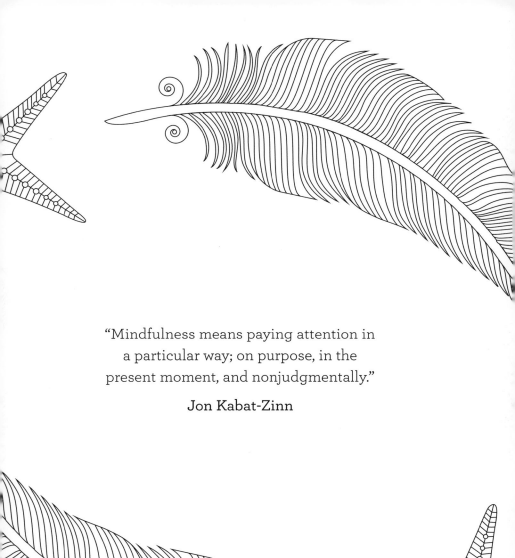

"Mindfulness means paying attention in a particular way; on purpose, in the present moment, and nonjudgmentally."

Jon Kabat-Zinn

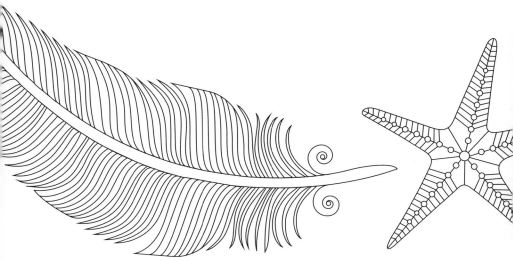

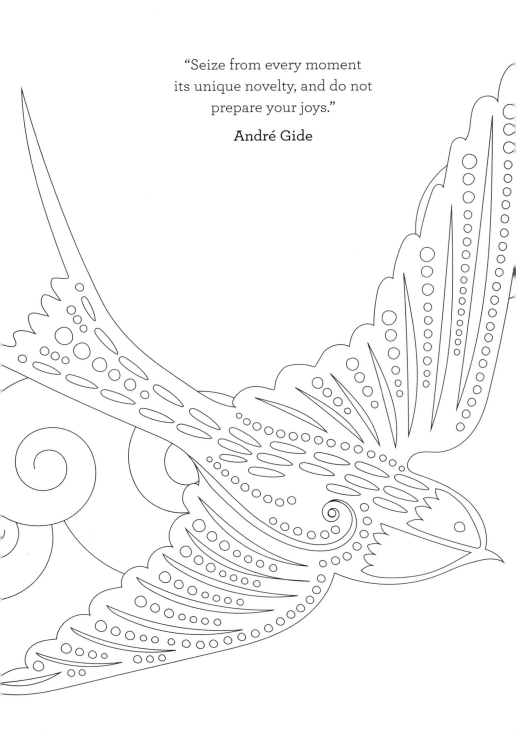

"Seize from every moment
its unique novelty, and do not
prepare your joys."

André Gide

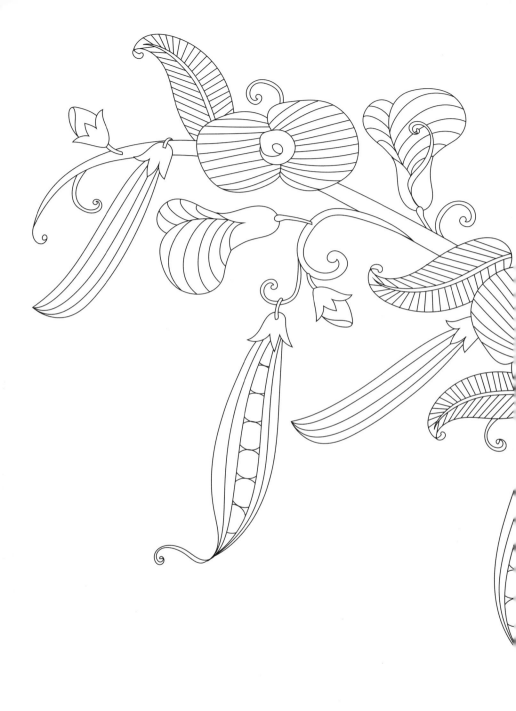

"What lies behind you and what lies
in front of you, pales in comparison
to what lies inside of you."

Ralph Waldo Emerson

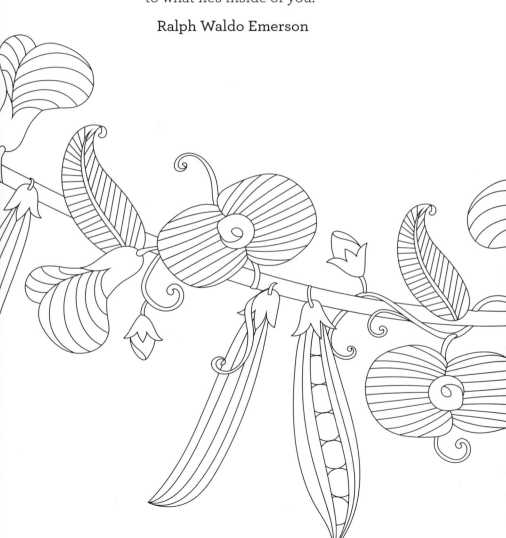

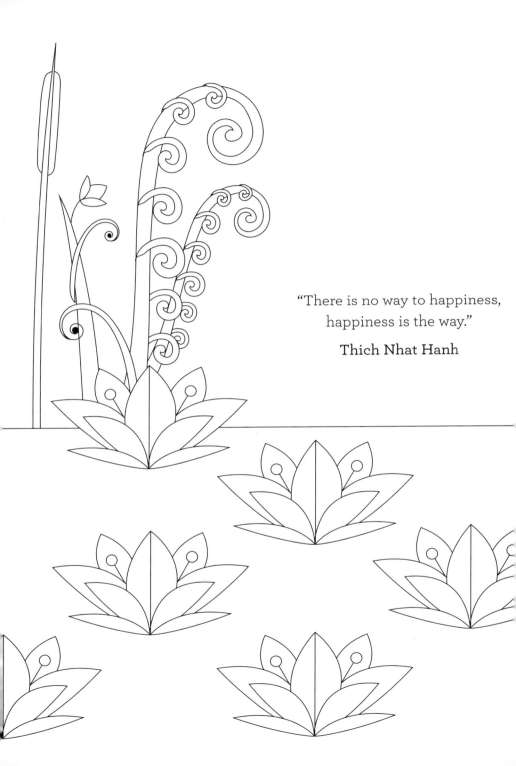

"There is no way to happiness,
happiness is the way."

Thich Nhat Hanh

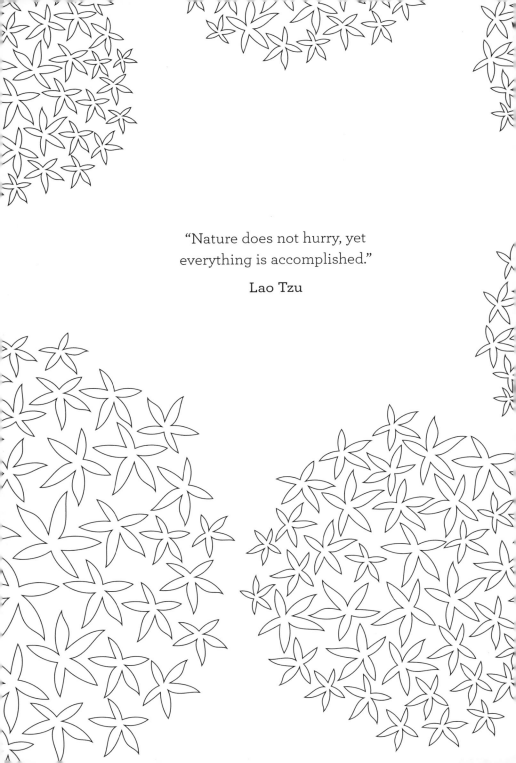

"Nature does not hurry, yet
everything is accomplished."

Lao Tzu

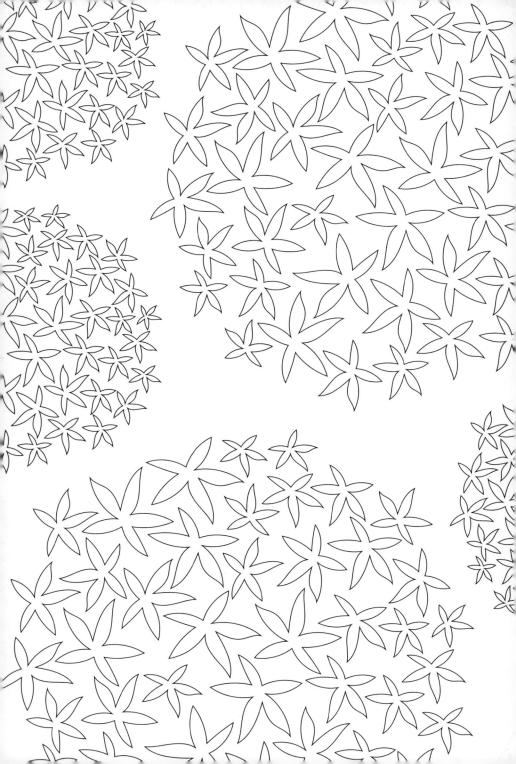

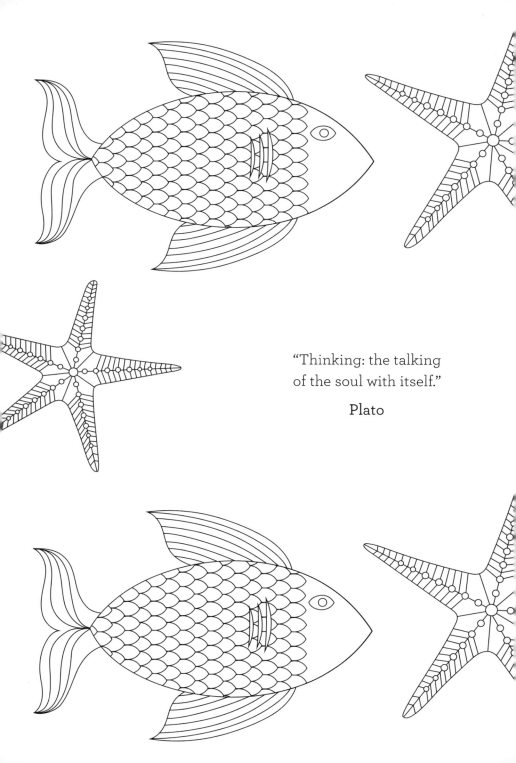

"Thinking: the talking of the soul with itself."

Plato

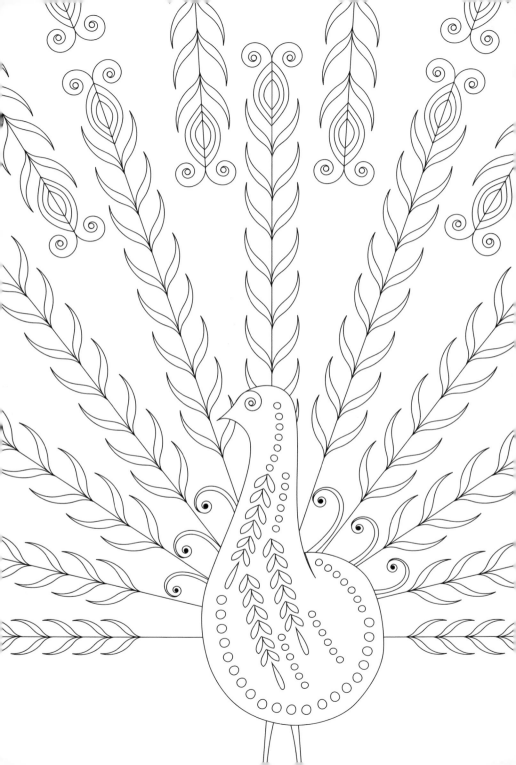

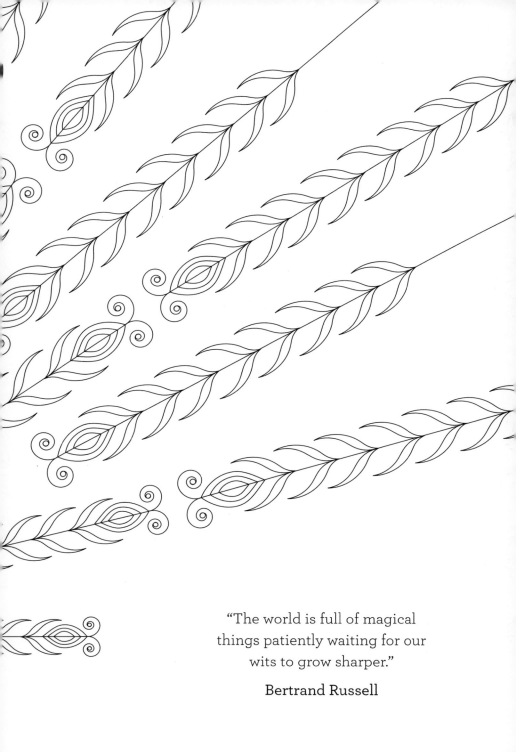

"The world is full of magical
things patiently waiting for our
wits to grow sharper."

Bertrand Russell

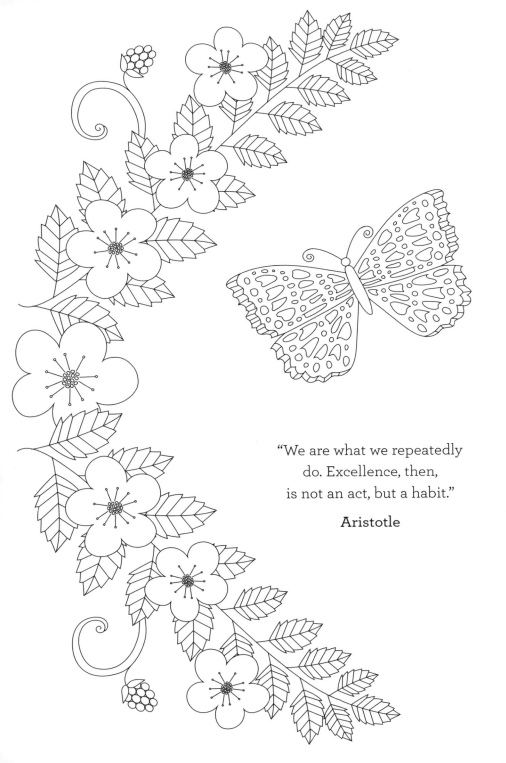

"We are what we repeatedly
do. Excellence, then,
is not an act, but a habit."

Aristotle

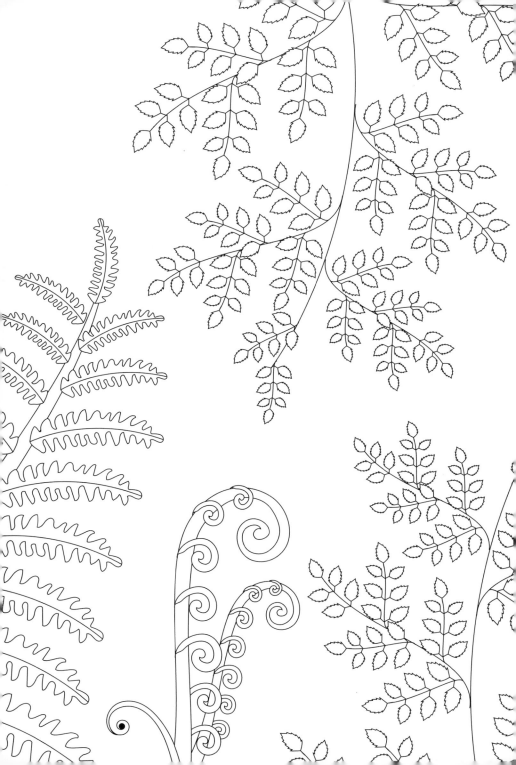

"Don't judge each day by the harvest you reap but by the seeds that you plant."

Robert Louis Stevenson

"Begin at once to live, and count each separate day as a separate life."

Seneca

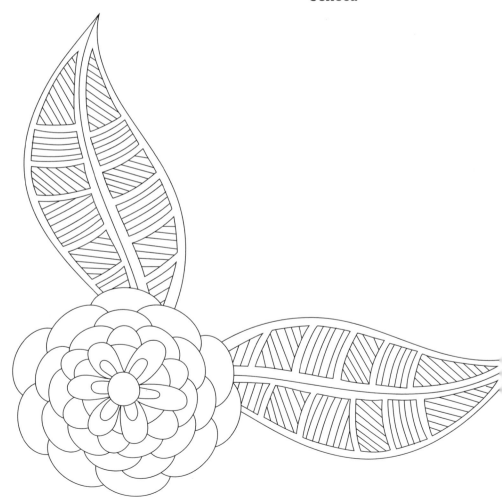

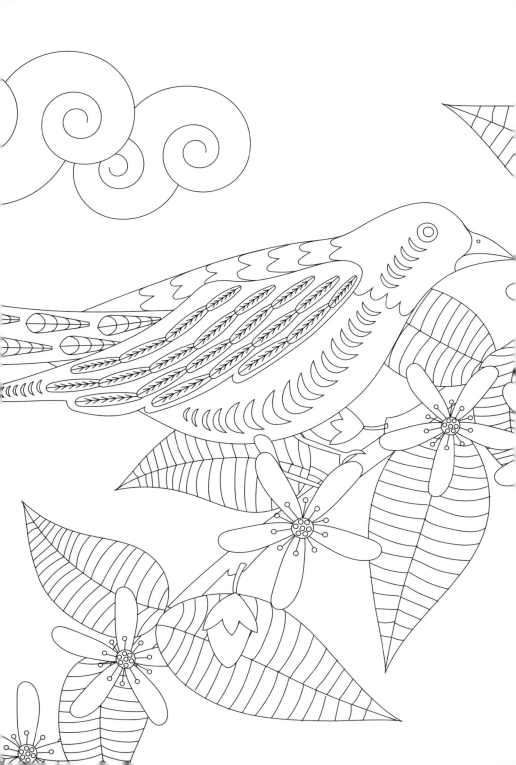

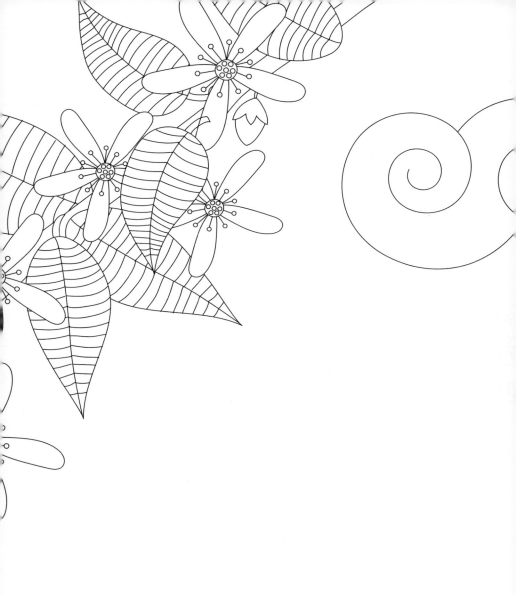

"What makes the desert beautiful
is that somewhere it hides a well"

Antoine de Saint-Exupery

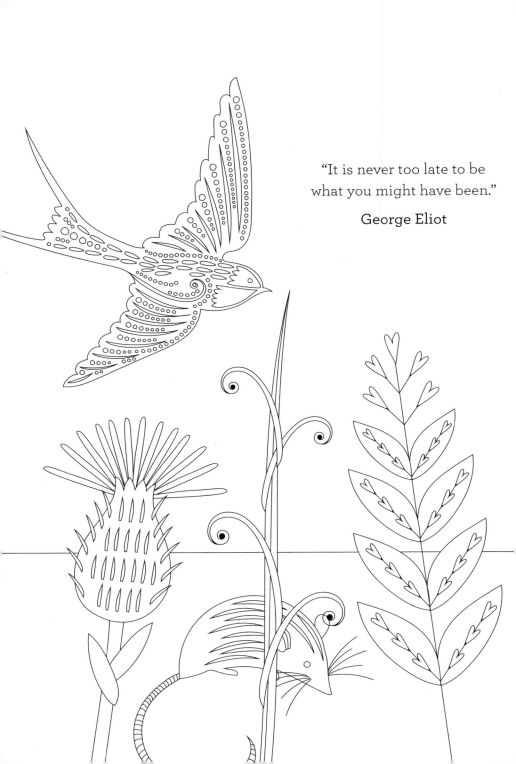

"It is never too late to be what you might have been."

George Eliot

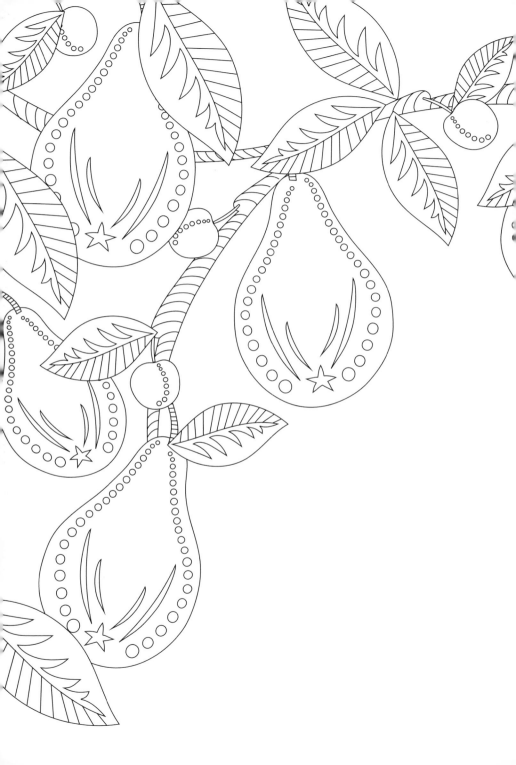

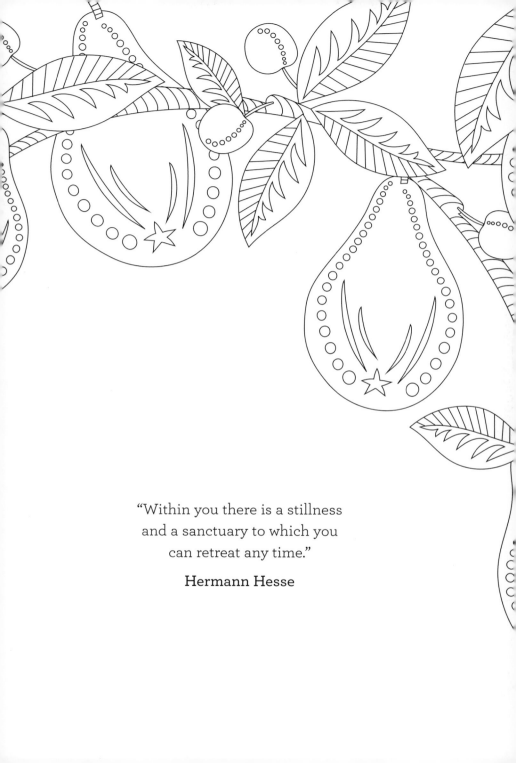

"Within you there is a stillness
and a sanctuary to which you
can retreat any time."

Hermann Hesse

"If we did all the things we are capable
of, we would astound ourselves."

Thomas A Edison

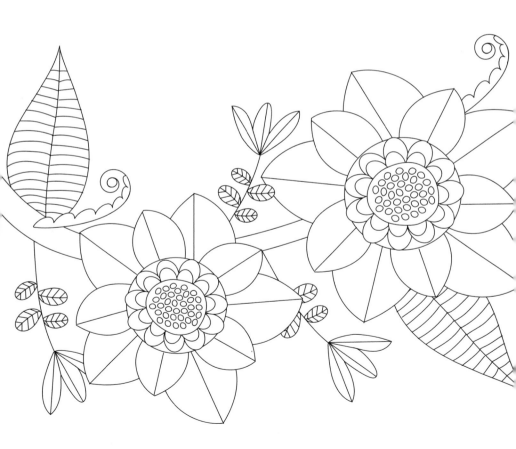

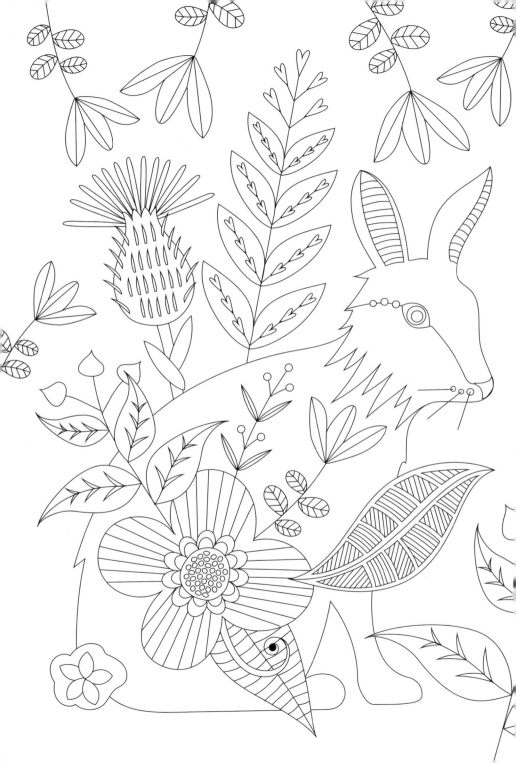

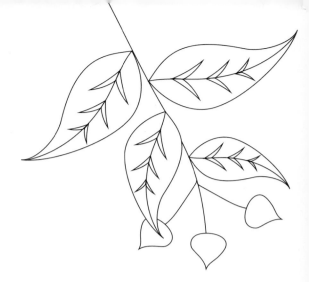

"Let every dawn be to you as the
beginning of life, and very setting
sun be to you as its close."

John Ruskin

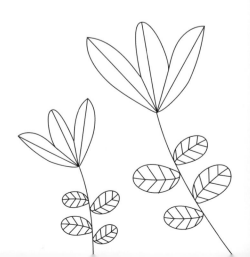

"Forever is composed of nows."

Emily Dickinson

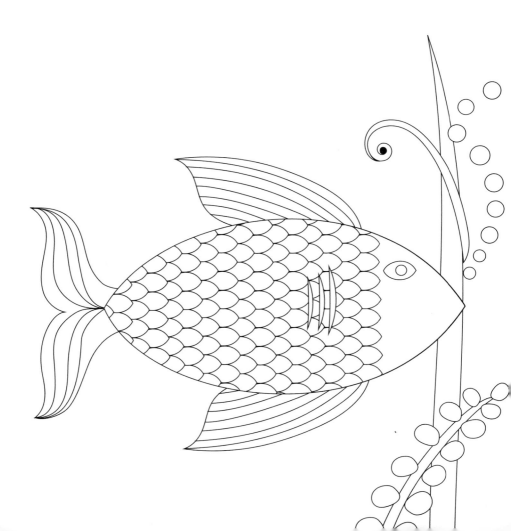

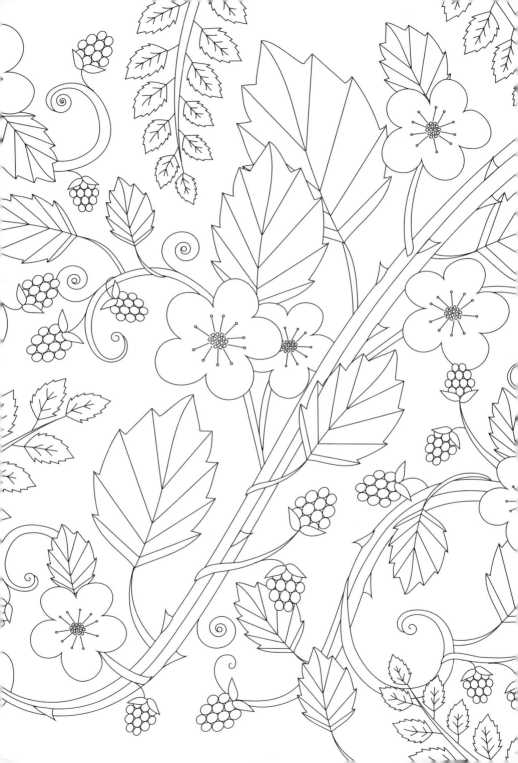

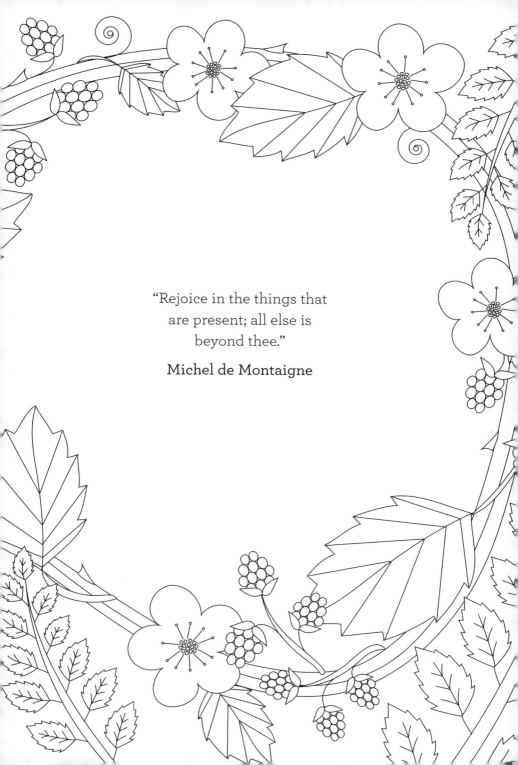

"Rejoice in the things that are present; all else is beyond thee."

Michel de Montaigne

"Do you have patience to wait till your mud settles and the water is clear? Can you remain unmoving till the right action arises by itself?"

Lao Tzu

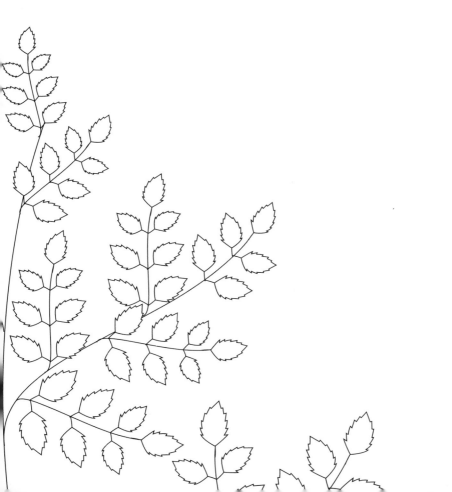

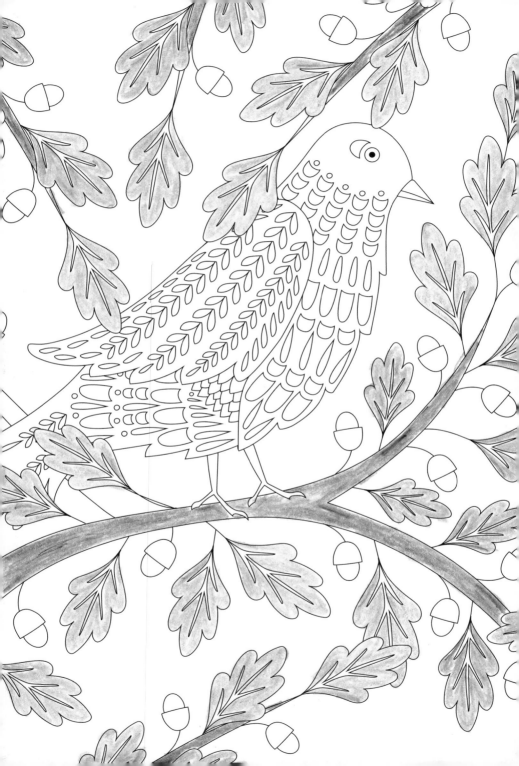

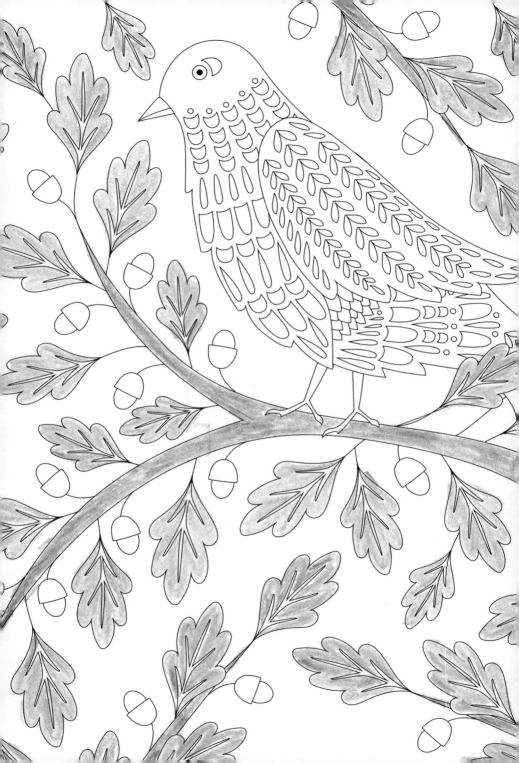

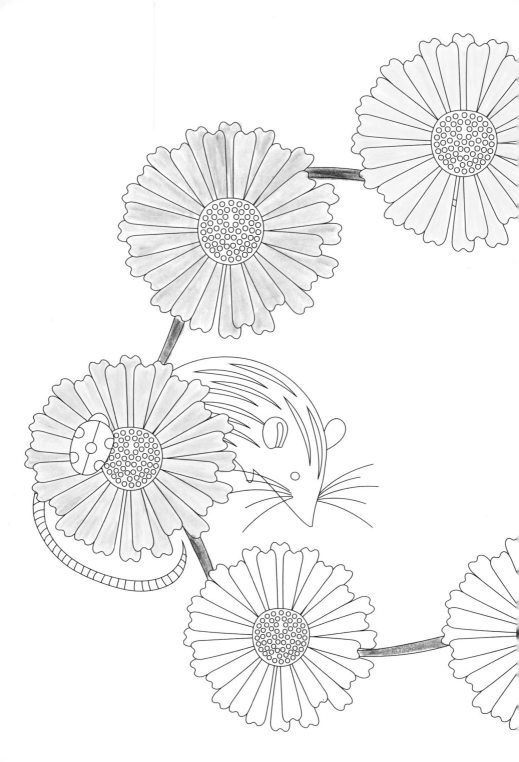